Creating a successful
e-information service

Also available by the authors

Griffiths, Peter, *Managing your internet and intranet services: the information and library professional's guide to strategy*, Library Association Publishing, 2000, ISBN 1 85604 340 1.

Pantry, Sheila, *Dealing with aggression and violence in your workplace*, Library Association Publishing, ISBN 1 85604 180 8 £12.50

Pantry, Sheila (ed.), *Building community information networks: strategies and experiences*, Library Association Publishing, 1999, ISBN 1 85604 337 1.

Pantry, Sheila and Griffiths, Peter, *Becoming a successful intrapreneur: a practical guide to creating an innovative information service*, Library Association Publishing, 1998, ISBN I 85604 292 8.

Pantry, Sheila and Griffiths, Peter, *The complete guide to preparing and implementing Service Level Agreements*, Library Association Publishing, 2001, 2nd edn, ISBN 1 85604 410 6.

Pantry, Sheila and Griffiths, Peter, *Developing a successful service plan*, Library Association Publishing, ISBN 1 85604 329 0.

Pantry, Sheila and Griffiths, Peter, *Your successful LIS career: planning your career, CVs, interviews and self-promotion*, Library Association Publishing, ISBN 1 85604 329 0

The Successful LIS Professional Series, edited by Sheila Pantry

Getting results with time management, by Ailsa Masterton, ISBN 1 85604 237 5, £12.50

Making project management work for you, by Liz McLachlan, ISBN 1 85604 203 0, £12.50

Managing your organization's records, by Elizabeth Parker, ISBN 1 85604 335 5, £13.50

Success at the enquiry desk, by Tim Owen, 3rd edn, ISBN 1 85604 404 1, £13.50

All titles available at 20% discount to CILIP members. Remember to quote your CILIP Membership Number if claiming the discount.

Available from Bookpoint Ltd, Mail Order Dept, 130 Milton Park, Abingdon, Oxon OX14 4SB, UK.
Tel: +44 (0)1235 827794; Fax: +44 (0)1235 400454;
e-mail: orders@bookpoint.co.uk

Creating a successful e-information service

Sheila Pantry OBE

Peter Griffiths

facet publishing

© Sheila Pantry and Peter Griffiths 2002

Published by
Facet Publishing
7 Ridgmount Street
London WC1E 7AE

Facet Publishing is wholly owned by CILIP: the Chartered Institute of Library and Information Professionals.

First published 2002

British Library Cataloguing in Publication Data

A catalogue record for this book is available from the British Library.

ISBN 1-85604-442-4

Peter Griffiths writes in a personal capacity but is grateful for the Home Office's agreement to publish his contribution to this book. Nothing in this text should be taken as a description of official practice, and mention of any commercial service or product does not imply any official endorsement.

Typeset in 11/15pt Aldine 401 BT and Syntax by Facet Publishing.
Printed and made in Great Britain by MPG Books Ltd, Bodmin, Cornwall.

CONTENTS

Introduction: Creating the Successful Electronic Information Service

Over the past 25 years or so information services have made increasing use of computers. Digital information tantalizes with exciting possibilities, but to realize the benefits fully information managers should understand the overall context of developing a totally electronic information service (EIS). We define an EIS as one where maximum use is made of electronically held information. Establishing an electronic information service from scratch may be easier than converting from a traditional paper-based service.

The library and information service (LIS) manager today continues to face many challenges in providing services that meet the requirements of all the customers of that service. In every sector of the information marketplace, the introduction and use of electronic information, new emphasis on value-for-money concepts and timeliness of information, coupled with downsizing and flatter management structure in organizations, have brought about significant changes.

A number of LIS managers have become experts in building and stocking virtual libraries. They have a high profile in the profession and many have considerable technical expertise as well as their library and information professional skills. Many of them are in large libraries, frequently but not exclusively in the academic sector, and for some of them a considerable part of their work forms part of one or more of the electronic library trials and projects now being conducted.

These digital library experts are working at the extreme frontier of progress – what we used to call the bleeding edge – and are dealing with problems (such as copyright licensing) in their own specialist environments. Their experience is deep and detailed, and while we may need to know what they have achieved, we do not necessarily need to know exactly how they did it. This is not least because the library and information landscape has some odd characteristics, one of which is that while problems may be common to a number of sectors, the solutions have to be different because of other factors. (Following the example, and as we shall see in the book, in the case of copyright licensing, the possible solutions vary as different conditions apply to different sectors as defined by third parties.) So what works on a university network serving thousands of students with licensed journal content may be interesting but impossible for a company information manager working on a network maintained by an external contractor and serving 2000 commercial researchers in three countries.

But what about these managers of LIS, who are not directly involved in this work but can see considerable potential value if it could be adapted to their own situation? How feasible is it for, say, the solo LIS manager working in a small company to introduce electronic services? Does it make any difference whether the company produces electrical goods or television programmes? How can a school librarian provide additional study facilities using e-library skills? What do you need to know, and which areas should you be monitoring to keep up to date with what is happening?

We shall not treat you to extensive descriptions of projects but we shall tell you that they are there, and where to go to keep abreast of new developments in the field. And we shall indicate the kinds of problem that others report finding as they go about making the case for the electronic library and e-information services in general.

After reading this book, we believe that you will at least be confident that you are aware of all the questions that need to be asked, even if you have to search further for the answers. You will have practical tips at hand to help you persuade those to whom electronic libraries are, so to speak, a closed book, and equally know how to begin to cope with enthusiastic senior managers who believe that all knowledge can be delivered at the push of a button, starting tomorrow.

Searching the literature has shown that there is still very little real guidance specifically aimed at the LIS practitioner about how to produce a total electronic information service. There is, as you can see in the bibliography, a wide range of articles on a number of relevant topics. But for the non-expert, who is faced with the need to create an EIS without the benefit of being part of one of the major centres of research and development of e-services, there is next to nothing in the way of advice on 'what works'. We hope that this book will help to close this gap in knowledge by providing useful ideas, hints and tips to be used when developing an EIS. We have drawn on personal experience, and knowledge of good examples.

Electronic services allow you to:

- enhance the services given to customers
- cut down on repetitive work
- maximize the stock available by holding information and documents in electronic form.

Each chapter is written to help you through the various stages of establishing your own electronic information service. Chapter 1 introduces the concept of the e-information service in which we give our definition and discuss the scope, the pluses and minuses of having just an e-information service, and how to change attitudes and perceptions from the traditional model to the new e-information model. We also discuss convergence and the difference information specialists/librarians make as intelligent filters, providing value added and non-work use plus 24/7 libraries (open 24 hours a day, 7 days a week). Chapter 2 looks at what an e-information service can offer to the various communities and the need for an information audit. Customers' needs, staff and their training and the costs are also discussed. Publicity, marketing and the business plan are all essential parts of creating the EIS and need to be understood. The whole reason for creating the EIS is the customer, and Chapter 3 addresses a host of questions including: who are the customers? Where are they located? Do they access information? Keeping the present customers as well as identifying new customers and the role of the information professional in customer e-service are covered.

Chapter 4 looks at the range and types of information needed in a number of areas such as general information, scientific, technical, medical, business and financial, legal and educational information. Other considerations include how often customers need information and the formats in which the information can be presented. No information service is an island and Chapter 5 looks at who needs to be involved in your plans both internally and externally, including contractors and suppliers.

What all this is going to cost is a major question and Chapter 6 looks at budgeting for your e-information service. We show how it is necessary to produce a business case and business plan, considering any dependencies within your organization and deciding whether to charge for services. Timescales are another essential problem to be mastered, as are measuring use of the service, and working together by considering library consortia for e-service purchasing: these are all a part of this chapter.

Once you have established your EIS you will need to keep in touch with the customers, evaluating and monitoring the services you offer, keeping yourself and your customers aware of developments in external suppliers' services. You will need to constantly check how any new services could meet your customers' needs and consider how to introduce these new services into your e-portfolio. Chapters 7 and 8 show you how to keep one step ahead of the competitors, identify your networks and be alert to what can they tell you.

For good measure we have added a glossary which shows some recent worldwide developments, and refers to several more in the associated reading list. Finally, for those of you curious to know more we have included an extensive reading list and list of websites to follow up.

Remember our maxim and keep asking yourself:

- Why are we providing this service?
- Should it be continued?
- Is there a better way?
- What should be provided?

- Is it really needed in the format provided?
- When is it done? Why then? Can a better time be found?
- Where is it done? Why there? Can a better place be found?
- Can someone else provide it?

Library and information services are vital to the well-being of organizations however small or large, whether in the private or public sector. By providing quality and appropriate services your electronic information service should succeed.

We wish you every success.

Sheila Pantry OBE and Peter Griffiths

1

INTRODUCING THE CONCEPT OF THE E-INFORMATION SERVICE

In this chapter you will find:

- our definition – what do we mean by an e-information service?
- the scope of e-information – what do e-services provide and who are the potential users?
- the pluses and minuses of introducing an e-information service
- how to change attitudes and perceptions from the traditional model to the new e-information model
- what is convergence – and why are universities going this way when corporate libraries increasingly contract out technical support to focus on Knowledge Management (KM) and Information Management (IM) as high profile in-house activities?
- the difference the information specialists/librarians make – their work as intelligent filters, providing added value
- non-work use and 24/7 information centres/ libraries: do they have an impact on the e-information service?

What do we mean by an e-information service?

Over the past 25 years or so, information services have made increasing use of computers. Electronic services allow the service to:

- enhance the services given to customers
- cut down on repetitive work
- maximize the stock available by holding information and documents in electronic forms.

Digital information technology holds out many tempting possibilities, but to realize the benefits fully information managers should understand the overall context of developing a totally electronic information service (EIS). We define an EIS as one where maximum use is made of electronically held information. Establishing an electronic information service from scratch may be easier than converting from a traditional paper-based service. In Chapters 2 and 4 we explore what kind of information service you may wish to provide, but we now need to look at the component parts of the electronic information service.

Library and information services (LIS – a term that we shall use throughout this book to indicate libraries, information centres or information services in whatever sector they may be, preferring 'library' or 'information centre' only when we discuss the specific type of service) have a wide range of electronic resources to choose from in order to make up the constituent parts of the EIS. Depending on the main subject area in which the LIS is operating, the following list suggests some of those choices:

- computer software
- standalone and network databases
- CD-ROMs
- electronic journals
- multimedia products
- image collections
- encyclopedias
- reference materials
- daily news
- access to financial information sources
- legislation
- scientific, technical and medical information.

Scope

To establish a successful EIS, it is essential that you define the scope of the service you are establishing. This will require strategic planning, including an information audit of needs of the customers and management, which will require consultation with customers, both current and potential. But without this foundation work, you will not establish a sound base for the service.

Your objective is to establish and ensure broad access to a wide range of resources. To do this it is essential that you co-ordinate the access given to the various parts of your organization, particularly in terms of licensing, and of the use of the electronic services, agreeing who may or may *not* use the resources. If your LIS is open to the public or to a number of large groups such as students and faculty, similar analysis will be needed. There are likely to be financial implications in your choice, possibly because of the funding arrangements for particular groups, or the licensing concessions available.

Defining your users

You will need to agree who the users are, so as to be able to cater adequately for their information needs now and in the future. A number of factors may influence the definition of a user of any LIS. This could be affected by agreements between your organization and others, for example agreements between local authorities, colleges or universities or businesses on a bilateral basis or as a consortium. For example in the South Yorkshire area of the UK registered open access ticket holders who live and work in the area can access all the libraries, information centres and learning centres of the local universities, colleges and public libraries. It becomes more difficult to define users, and particularly the rights they acquire through being users, when the definition lies around an organization such as a company or a college rather than a geographic area. As we shall see, licensing rules may make it impossible to provide full services to distance learners because of the rules imposed by the rights owners. So, not only may we find some potential users excluded, but there may be different classes of user within the same organization.

Here, for example, are some of the possible groupings of users for some of the major LIS sectors. Each will have particular requirements for potential components of an EIS, and the conditions of use of the service must cater for those groups.

Users in the academic sector

- university faculty staff
- students – on campus (undergraduate, postgraduate, doctoral)
- students – off campus (e.g. accessing university network by dial-up from local area)
- distance learning students
- disadvantaged staff and students
- research workers located elsewhere
- consultants
- information seekers who are not affiliated to the university.

Users of public libraries

- members of the public, including children
- people who work in the area
- businesses
- researchers
- users of specified collections
- distance learning students.

Users of private sector information services

- own staff, in principal business premises
- own staff, in other business premises (e.g. overseas offices)
- own staff, on business travel (e.g. dial-up from clients' premises or hotel)
- users from other information centres and libraries belonging to a local

co-operative with whom there is a reciprocal agreement may also be granted use – perhaps in a limited way

- consultants or secondees working for the company or organization (i.e. employees of other organizations on the company's premises).

Users of government information services

- own department or agency staff
- researchers working for the department or agency
- other government departments' or agencies' staff
- consultants
- general public.

Some of these groups will contain users who wish to find information in order to republish it, e.g. in research documents or as journalism. This will also have an impact on the level of service that can be offered.

Pluses and minuses

What are the positive and negative aspects of building an EIS?

Before you embark on the consultation and information audit stage you must have a clear understanding of the positive and negative issues in establishing an EIS. Unconvinced players are certain to ask you to list the benefits to be gained, and to consider the disbenefits (the issues to be tackled before the benefits can be realized). You must be ready with answers that demonstrate a sound and cost-effective argument for the service. When you list these, you could finish with a chart something like the following.

Pluses

- better access to a wider range of information
- potential to provide better value for money, e.g. by entering into

5

consortium buying agreements for e-services (although overall costs may be higher)
- better use of staff time
- less time spent on housekeeping manual sources
- potential to provide 24/7 access without having to have large numbers of staff present
- total stock access without any risk of losing physical documents, e.g. issues of journals
- equal access to stock – e.g. everyone able to see the current issue of a journal
- potential to reduce or eliminate multiple purchase where electronic access is possible (and multiple use can be licensed).

Minuses

- costs – investment in technology and other start-up costs, additional licence fees
- savings may not be realized if paper subscriptions have to be kept (e.g. where a paper subscription must be bought to gain access to e-content)
- staff may not have the necessary negotiating skills to get maximum benefits from agreements
- reliance on technologies that may 'go down' and disconnect all users – hence the need for reliable and robust systems (and perhaps to store paper copies off-site or have reciprocal back-up agreements!)
- staff may require additional skills (and hence training) to be able to perform their duties
- users also may not have the basic technological skills to be able to get maximum benefits from an electronic information service – using a computer is less intuitive than reading a book!

The chart you compile will reflect the position in your particular organization. Some of these issues are generic and will probably apply wherever you are. There will be other issues that only apply to your situation, maybe about the technology system or the availability of online information services in your key subject fields. Whatever they are, by having a sound plus and minus list you will be able to present an effective argument, demonstrating the benefits of an EIS, as well as acknowledging possible drawbacks.

Auditing the electronic service requirement

The final shape of the EIS will depend on the requirements that you establish. Although you will probably have a good idea of the subject information requirements – and our checklists on information audit (Pantry and Griffiths, 1998 and 2002) will help if you do not – your users will need some help in identifying how their needs can be met from electronic sources. A checklist of available services drawn from up-to-date monitoring of the e-publishing industry (and here your suppliers will probably support you) will help your users to identify their information requirements, and to assess the services that potentially match them.

A checklist such as the one that follows overleaf will prompt your users to identify their needs from the range of available services that you will offer. Amend it to suit your own situation.

XXX Information Services	Service	Training
The following services may be offered:	requested	needed

1 Computer software
 • [names of specific software available in the
  EIS, e.g. word-processing software].

2 Standalone and networked databases
 • CD-ROMs [e.g. newspapers and financial]
 • LIS catalogue and bulletins

3 Electronic journals

4 Multimedia products
 • CD-ROMs [e.g. training courses on disc]

5 Image collections

6 Encyclopedias

7 Other reference materials
 • maps, country, city and towns
 • postcode finder
 • address finder

8 Daily news
 • BBC
 • ITN
 • Ananova
 • Newswires, e.g. PA News
 • CNN

9 Access to financial information sources

10 Legislation
 • UK Acts and SIs
 • European legislation
 • *Hansard, Official Journal*, etc.

11 Scientific, technical and medical information

Managing change

You will find in the consultation period that you frequently hear the same debates and arguments repeated – whether to object to or support your proposals. Your own users may well be your biggest helpers in managing change with their ideas and comments. Take note of what they say and share their positive thinking if you need to convince others. What are likely to be the major issues? Some of these may be on your list.

- People may ask what was wrong with the old service. Be prepared to explain that rising costs and growing pressure on space are among the reasons that change simply has to happen in many organizations.
- Many people do not like change and prefer the 'comfort blanket' of paper-based information services. You will need to demonstrate the higher quality of service being offered through your improvements.
- In many organizations, delivery of information using electronic services is a distinctly experimental business. There may be some nervousness as well as resistance to change.
- You are certain to find that there is a range of technical abilities among users, some having advanced knowledge of systems and services, and others just the basic skills. Be prepared to help those whose skills need reinforcing to take full advantage, and those who may be experts in building Access databases but discover that their search skills are not as sharp as they thought!
- Timid users of the service may be scared off by the appearance of a large amount of new equipment in the LIS, particularly if much of the familiar paper stock disappears at the same time.

There is an impression that enthusiasm for electronic services declines as the age of the user increases. But this has nothing to do with age: some older people have embraced electronic systems, while many others (of all ages) will avoid using such systems and services at all costs. Often it emerges that potential users have no real idea of their aptitude for using information. The discussions you have with users should uncover their training needs. The

LIS should be more than ready to offer training as part of winning people over, making them competent and efficient in their work.

You should never be surprised by what your enquiries reveal about how people work. The now classic response from a director, when asked by one of us 'Do you use electronic mail?' was 'Yes, most definitely, my secretary prints off the message, I hand write on it the answer, and she sends it off'!

How to change attitudes and perceptions from the traditional model to the new e-information model

So much for the approaches to building an EIS and the elements that might appear in planning for such a service. But why should any organization want to move in this direction when the traditional model seems to continue to meet so many people's needs?

Case studies

Digital reference service in the new millennium: planning, management and evaluation (Lankes, Collins and Kasowitz, 2000) provides examples of what is happening, and indeed of what has happened already in the USA. Digital reference can no longer be considered the future of information services: in fact, it is already here and is likely to become a mainstay of electronic and networked services. Many users believe that 'It is all there on the internet and free', but the attendant cynical reaction to this statement from information professionals is entirely justified.

The authors of the book have been involved in the pioneering Virtual Reference Desk Project (**www.vrd.org**) and the associated Virtual Reference Desk Digital Conference. Theirs have been among the foremost efforts to better understand and use digital reference tools in a networked environment. They show how the notion of 24/7 (24 hours a day, 7 days a week) digital reference services and electronic information services opens the way for innovative services.

These facilities offer information professionals new opportunities to provide remote reference services to their users and the general public and to set standards for high-quality information services. Reference specialists will *not* become extinct or an endangered species, but the emergence of digital and distributed information environments have temporarily unhinged a relationship that has been stable for the past hundred years or so. Users are adopting new information-seeking behaviour, so that information managers, reference specialists and knowledge managers must now forge new kinds of relationships with users. Technology is providing the opportunities to create a 'renaissance reference culture' based on these new relationships. Following the example of Amazon.com, whose 'push' technology can identify titles of potential interest to its customers, LIS need to adopt technology that can identify what kind of services, databases, subject categories, etc. are in demand by users.

Convergence – giving technical skills to librarians and information skills to technical staff

What do we mean by convergence? Around 15 years ago, librarians first commented on the growing overlap of library service tasks with the work of other areas of the organization, and that there was a trend towards co-location in organizational or geographic terms. The most frequent partner in this merger was the computer section, and many information staff and librarians have become very competent in the technical field, to such an extent that they have been able to rise to heights in an organization's structure never achieved before by the information professional. But information specialists are now taking on wider knowledge management and information management roles within the framework of the converged service, making them even more central to their organization, and reflecting the continuing move away from marginalization of the LIS.

The trend to convergence is most frequently encountered in the academic sector but it is now happening in many sectors – government, finance, law, private companies, institutions and associations.

The gradual automation of library tasks, followed in the last few years by the apparent automation of many information retrieval tasks through use of the internet, has led to a gradual blurring of the roles and boundaries of the library professional and the information technology professional. The older relationship between the two functions will no longer do. Library computing is carried out on systems that are effectively under the control of the library itself rather than a central computing service whose task was formerly to maintain a hall full of mainframe computers. The computing function increasingly offers direct access to information sources without playing an intermediary role, or acting as interpreter or quality assessor for that information. Who does what? Whose responsibility lies where?

So far as many academic organizations are concerned, the obvious answer seems to be to bring the library within a wider body with a title such as 'learning development' or 'academic services'. In corporate organizations the term 'information services' or 'information systems' is widely interpreted to mean 'computer services'. In local government a different kind of convergence seems to have taken place where libraries and other leisure services have been bundled into a leisure services department; but there is less obvious overlap of function here.

One paper on the subject of convergence (Shapiro and Long, 1994) in the academic sector comments simply that the time for turf wars is over. It makes the point that in order to survive, the library and the computer centre need each other, and their skills are complementary. In practice, the issue is how best use can be made of resources and skills in order to meet demand that is ever increasing and ever more complex. Urgency is given to the problem because the available budgets are under increasing pressure. Competition between the library and the computer service for money to do the same job is likely to end with neither being satisfied, and the funds going to a third party.

How does this work in practice?

In one university library in the London area of the UK, long opening hours have created a requirement for basic information services and technical support to be provided over an extended working day. The service desk has become the focus of this converged service, and a staff training programme has been initiated for all team members who work on this desk. While detailed technical or information enquiries are deferred until core hours on the following working day, desk staff have basic skills in both library and information work and in computer services. Thus they can advise on the range of information sources available in the library and locate basic resources, as well as being able to fix simple technical faults and maintain electronic equipment (such as resetting computers and printers, and restoring failed connections).

There is a clear recommendation in this case that frontline staff need to be competent in both areas of work. There may be some managerial issues to be faced, particularly over the level of enquiry that technical (i.e. non-LIS qualified) staff will be allowed to handle. However there is generally less concern over the technical skills that librarians now require, and the level of expertise required is likely to fall easily within the capabilities of many library and information professionals, particularly new graduates. What both groups may need is training for training – that is, the ability to put across their technical skills in such a way that users can learn what to do on a future occasion rather than calling for help.

Similar solutions have been found to these problems in other countries. In Australia many university libraries now accept this change as a way of life; it has been emerging at least since the mid-1990s (Sayers, 1999). In the USA, the earliest commentators were addressing this problem in the mid-1980s, and using the term 'converge' to describe the process (Moholt, 1985).

These requirements are probably true across all kinds of library and information service. In public libraries, staff are often faced with technical problems outside the standard five-day working week. Other areas of work, such as web services, report that if problems occur at the start of a weekend the library may lose several hours of service before technical staff are available to handle a helpdesk call. The ability of staff to fix at least the more simple faults is especially important for branches located in rural areas, as here there is often no acceptable alternative service within easy reach of the library patron (Griffiths, 2000).

Corporate libraries are likely to enjoy the support of a central computer department, but must recognize that their software and other information services are unlikely to be seen as the most important element of the network. Third-party suppliers may well be involved (in the form of library automation suppliers or database providers) and negotiations with these suppliers may have to be through a central helpdesk that is unfamiliar with library services. The corporate intranet may well use the same protocols as information providers used by the corporate information centre, but there may be additional problems with external firewalls and other barriers to easy and seamless communication. The library's technical staff may need to use their skills of negotiation to get their requirements taken seriously by the technical team, particularly where these appear to conflict with the core network.

Convergence is likely to raise a number of management issues that need to be resolved. You may not have an immediate answer to some of the following points, but it would be as well to consider them.

The divide between professional and para-professional staff becomes problematic, and needs to be defined fairly carefully. At what level of complexity does an enquiry need to be referred higher? This can be tricky to decide, because the decision may rely not only on the difficulty of the enquiry but the time of day at which it is put.

It may be easier (and more effective) to create a new team with the required skills mix, rather than trying to re-train existing staff with a broader mix of lower-level skills than they may currently possess. What skills are in fact essential? A core skill set must be defined and published, providing a point of reference for new staff and old and helping to define the higher level of skills needed to tackle advanced library or information technology tasks.

What impression is given to users of your services by your approach to promoting them and even to naming them?

As we noted earlier, many people still do not understand the way that library and information professionals use the word 'information', and that e-service appears to be delivered by computer with little intervention by 'librarians'. So, how do you want the service to appear?

As we saw above, convergence has now gone beyond the simple union of LIS and its information technology support services. We are also witnessing many corporate organizations contracting out their IT services to the independent sector who provide IT and ASP services remotely and even staff them remotely, with advice provided by helpline services.

Outsourcing, as writers such as Charles Handy (1989) remind us, allows the main organization to concentrate on the core business, and it is reflected in patterns of employment, the shift in demand for cerebral rather than manual skills, and in the virtual disappearance of life-long, full-time jobs. New types of de-structured organizations arise, requiring new skills and new approaches. Handy called this 'the Shamrock organization' where the core people and work are kept within the organization and the rest of the work is contracted out.

In terms of information provision, organizations like this can be difficult to service within the conditions often imposed in contracts and agreements. At the same time these corporate organizations are recognizing the value of keeping Knowledge Management (KM) and Information Management (IM) as increasingly high profile in-house activities. This is because knowledge workers, with their skills of information and IT management, know how to capture, filter, store and retrieve information, while at the time they watch the information industry developments and services and they can identify which offerings are pertinent to the organization.

The growth of Knowledge Manager and Information Manager posts advertised and filled in the past few years shows the success that these managers are having within the organization. In the USA, according to a recent report, the demand for senior level librarians, now often known as chief information officers, is growing rapidly. As the corporate sector grows, there is a brain drain from other sectors such as academic libraries, which are now finding it difficult to keep experienced information professionals.

The difference the information professional makes – an intelligent filter, a creator of added value

Over the years the role and value of having information staff has been heavily debated. But the current view is that there has never been a better time for the information professional. Many attribute this boost to the growth of the internet, which has caused an information explosion, although as we saw above, this is not an entirely accurate view.

There is a huge demand for professionals with a solid management background, internet experience – especially website building – strong research and analytical skills, staff management experience and an understanding of the employing organization's industry sector. All these are to be found in the ranks of information-trained professionals.

The difference which the information professionals make to an organization is that they bring intelligent filters to the job. Information professionals add value to the employing organization.

Non-work use and 24/7 information centres/libraries: do they have an impact on the e-information service?

If your proposed EIS includes the internet, your service has the potential to put a new resource that is open to misuse on the desk of everyone in the organization. The debate continues as to whether use of the information service for non-work activities, such as personal hobbies and interests, is legitimate. In a number of organizations misuse of the internet is a sacking offence, and there have been a number of high-profile cases in recent months. Many commentators strongly advise organizations to devise, publish and maintain a policy on the use of the internet; this should cover use of e-mail as well as the web. The LIS cannot act in isolation, and however altruistic it may be in providing access to electronic information services the organization's own policies and politics must be adhered to. The LIS must incorporate the parent organization's rules into the regulations for use of the EIS.

Because of the ease of ordering from online suppliers, make it publicly clear that you will not accept responsibility for information materials that are ordered from the internet without the agreement of the LIS. This is an extension of the procurement policies that should exist in any soundly run organization, and should not cause outcry. Similarly, make it clear which websites the LIS recommends (if any) and provide warnings about the use of information found on other sites without corroborating evidence.

The LIS could find its policies challenged if there are any awkward cases that involve the use of electronic services within the organization. This can be a difficult situation for the EIS manager. Such incidents should not be used as an excuse for the organization to restrict the use of electronic information services, but the problem must be tackled by technical means (such as blocking access to some websites through software) or managerial means (such as running awareness courses where the severity of the offence is made clear). There is no good reason why information services for the benefit of the majority should be lost through the action of a few people (and, arguably, the inaction of their managers).

Summary

You will now understand our definition for this book of an e-information service and the scope of e-information, including what e-services can be provided and who are the potential users. You will have an understanding of the pluses and minuses of introducing an e-information service, as well as ways to change attitudes and perceptions from the traditional model to the new e-information model.

This introduction also gives an understanding about convergence and why universities are going this way while corporate libraries increasingly contract out technical support to focus on Knowledge Management (KM) and Information Management (IM) as high profile in-house activities. Most of all you will understand the difference information specialists/librarians make in their work as intelligent filters, providing added value. Lastly you will have an appreciation about non-work use and 24/7 information centres/libraries, and the impact an e-information service can make on an organization.

2

WHAT KIND OF AN E-INFORMATION SERVICE DO YOU WANT TO PROVIDE?

An information service must meet the needs of the user community, and this applies as much to an EIS as to other information services. The style of service that you provide will depend on a number of factors that we consider here.

In this chapter we look at:

- what an e-information service can offer
- the organization's (or the community's) needs
- information audit and consultancy
- customer needs
- the 24/7 e-information service
- staff and their training
- business planning.

What an e-information service can offer

In Chapter 1 we saw that an electronic information service is one where there is maximum use of electronically held information, and we indicated some of the services that could be given. We now explore some options for the type of information services you might choose to provide.

Electronic information services typically offer facilities such as those in the following range of resources. The consultation and information audit exercise will indicate what your users would value most.

Electronic journals

Increasing numbers of journals are published simultaneously or even exclusively on the internet. Many EIS manage their purchase through one of the several subscription agents that operate nationally and internationally. The services they provide include contents page alert, full-text articles, and access to archive searching for back issues. Agents are increasingly dealing with purchasing consortia, which provide cost benefits for both the suppliers and purchasers. We look at these consortia in more detail in the last section of Chapter 6.

Electronic books

Although less commonly found than electronic journals, the e-book is becoming a viable means of book publication. The rise in popularity of personal digital assistants (PDAs) has allowed a stable technical platform to be used which allows users to download books or chapters that can be read away from the office or home, while services such as e-brary offer the opportunity to purchase access to small sections of text as well as longer extracts.

Standalone and networked databases and CD-ROMs

There will be a number of databases and CD-ROMs, compiled by the information centre or by various departments or bought in from external sources, which should be available over the local network, or on a standalone workstation within the LIS.

Multimedia products, image collections, encyclopedias, reference materials

The EIS can construct a 'Reference Shelf' of electronic information using a variety of sources such as encyclopedias, handbooks, maps of towns and cities, postcode and address finders.

Daily news

Depending upon the needs of the users, links can be made to a variety of web-based news services such as the BBC, CNN and other news providers. A number of enhanced news feeds are available at a fee, such as those provided by the major news agencies.

Access to financial information sources

Some of this is free while others are fee-based services. Again the consultation and information audit will have revealed what kind of information is needed and how often.

In both the above examples, it may be possible to use a feed from the broadcast version of the services to provide streaming video and audio on the network. In a business organization this can be supplemented by locally generated video content.

Legislation

There are now daily updates for UK and European legislation services, which offer the full text of the acts, statutory instruments, directives, decisions and commentary. Texts of non-European countries' legal codes and commentaries are also readily available; portals such as FindLaw (**www.findlaw.com**) allow rapid location of a range of useful resources.

Computer software

There are many opportunities, particularly if the information service also runs the computer section, to offer a range of software packages to suit your users' everyday needs. Alongside the availability of the software the EIS could also offer, perhaps in conjunction with the training department, various levels of training to enable the user to make better use of the full facilities offered in these packages.

Organizational needs

An important task for information managers is to get a clear understanding of the entire organization or community in which the service will operate. Without this understanding the information service will not achieve a central role in the user community. An LIS that is driven by a vision shared only by its own staff will never be seen as important by the organization it serves.

Irrespective of the subject background, the organization's or the community's needs should be identified and captured before work begins on the design and creation of the service, or the identification of the electronic components within it. The first step is to carry out an information audit of the organization's information needs.

Information audit and consultancy

An information audit provides the organization with a wealth of important data such as:

- what information exists within the organization
- where it is located
- what information the organization needs and when it is needed
- who uses it
- what gaps exist
- where potential customers for information are in the organization

- why people use a particular service or source of information in preference to others
- why some people use the service frequently or occasionally
- why some people never use the service
- how to produce the information in the format needed.

Armed with this data, the LIS manager can begin to put together the range of services that will meet the needs of the greatest number of users in the most cost-effective way. But remember that it can take considerable time from initial consultation and information audit to the final outcomes in the form of revised services. An exercise carried out at the Royal College of Nursing was reported recently to have taken a full two years (Hyams, 2001).

To obtain the data, the LIS manager should hold discussions with managers or other representatives (depending on the type of community being served) to gather details of the types of information that members of that community need. One effective means of doing this is by using a standardized proforma. We provide an example overleaf to consider (Table 2.1). The exercise should provide a clear understanding of the ways that users currently access information, and of the types of information that they use.

As well as revealing what kind of information is needed, who needs it, and the range of topics that must be covered, your proforma will also show requirements for any kind of information that is not currently available in the organization. It may also disclose software packages and other systems that are being used in one or other part of the community to good effect but that are not available throughout the organization. The audit questionnaire will also identify any regular specialist information needs together with systems and service being used to meet those requirements.

Most organizations possess a wealth of information, but it is spread across the various departments or teams, or it rests with individual staff members who do not share it with others. Senior managers often hold the key to uncovering needs and resources. Typical questions and activities that can help them to identify these include:

Table 2.1 *A standardized proforma*

Section 1: Information requirements - business managers	Publications	Offical publications	Universities (research results, etc)	Government departments and agencies	Other organizations	Trades bodies	Research organizations	Business television	Broadcast television	Online data	Internet	Internal sources
Legislation	X	X				X	X				X	X
Stock prices								X		X	X	
Financial data				X				X		X	X	
Statistics	X	X		X							X	X
Newspaper articles and comment	X			X			X			X	X	
Companies House data		X		X	X					X	X	
Newsletters and journals	X		X		X		X				X	X
Conference papers	X		X	X	X		X				X	X
Literature reviews	X		X		X		X					
Specifications	X	X	X	X			X				X	
Videos	X		X		X			X	X		X	
Books	X	X	X	X	X		X					
CD-ROM	X	X	X	X	X	X	X					
Codes of practice	X	X					X				X	X
Health and safety information		X		X		X	X				X	X

Section 2: Current sources of information	Publications	Offical publications	Universities (research results, etc)	Government departments and agencies	Other organizations	Trades bodies	Research organizations	Business television	Broadcast television	Online data	Internet	Internal sources
Professional groups	X				X	X					X	X
Libraries, etc	X	X	X	X	X	X	X					
Personal collections	X	X	X	X	X	X						
Personal contacts		X	X	X	X	X	X	X	X		X	X
External suppliers	X	X	X	X	X	X	X			X	X	
Media								X	X		X	X
Government departments / agencies		X		X	X		X				X	X
Universities	X		X		X		X			X	X	X

Section 3: Means of distributing information	Senior management	Middle management	Finance directorate	Research directorate	Production line	Logistics section	Office staff	Publicity staff	External customers
Newspapers	X	X	X	X				X	X
Newsletters	X	X	X	X	X	X	X	X	X
Journals	X	X	X	X				X	X
Books	X	X	X	X				X	X	X
Abstracts bulletin	X	X	X	X		X	X		X
SDI / SCANS / CASIAS	X	X	X	X					
Translations	X	X		X			X	X	
Video recordings	X	X			X	X		X	X
Audio recordings	X	X	X	X				X	X
Intranet	X	X	X	X	X	X	X	X	
Web site	X	X	X	X			X	X	X
Extranet									X
Streaming video / audio	X	X	X	X	X	X	X	X	
Campaigns	X	X	X	X	X	X	X	X	X
Exhibitions					X	X	X	X	X
Conferences and seminars	X	X	X	X					X
Fax distribution					X	X		X	X
e-Mail distribution	X	X	X	X	X	X	X	X	X
CD-ROM presentations					X	X	X		X
Computer databases	X	X	X	X	X	X	X		X
Software programs			X	X	X	X	X		

- Which information resources do you believe support the organization's aims and objectives and its programme of work (or the community's activities or whatever is a relevant version of this question)? For a commercial concern, what information supports its products and its markets?
- Can you categorize these information sources into the following groups: essential; desirable; or nice to have?
- Where are the gaps in existing information flows and currently held information?
- As well as these gaps, what other major information needs exist?
- How many different computer-based information systems are in use already?
- How many people in the community use externally based information services already, e.g. online databases, the internet, CD-ROMs?

25

- Are all community members fully trained and able to use the computerized services and technologies?
- If not, how much training is needed and at what level?
- Finally, ask individuals the question: 'On what information do you depend to carry out your job, (or any regular activity in this community)?'

Problems

The information audit is likely to reveal a number of problems to be tackled. The following are commonly found, although you may find others that are specific to your organization or community:

- Information is power – so there may be a limited sharing of information. In an organization, sections or departments may hoard information, but it can easily be individuals in a community or corporate body who do this without involving others, even if they work in the same area.
- Sections and individuals may have developed databases but have not taken a co-ordinated approach. Information may be fragmented as a result, or else duplicated without it always being apparent that this has happened.
- Out-of-date information may be being used; or likewise information that has not been checked for validity and authority.
- Worse, an organization or community may be paying to acquire out-of-date information without realizing that it is inaccurate and largely valueless.
- Members of the community may suffer telecommunications problems such as a lack of e-mail facilities.
- Staff may lack training in information skills.
- A community may acquire the same or closely similar information several times over through lack of co-ordination between various groups of actors.

Defining information resources and services

In our recently revised book, *The complete guide to preparing and implementing service level agreements* (Pantry and Griffiths, 2001), we urged the use of a glossary or other agreed list of definitions to avoid any question of ambiguity over the questions asked in the audit and the interpretation. In the context of electronic information services, the areas detailed below will need particular attention. We have found considerable evidence that many managers understand neither the issues that information professionals have to deal with in purchasing and managing information, nor the terminology we use to describe those activities. The problem is that as information professionals we often seek the endorsement of other managers for our activities, when they do not understand the consequences of what we seek to do. Imagine the situation reversed: would you sanction a major re-organization of a financial or legal service if you had no idea what the service was providing because the description was ambiguous or meaningless, or couched in financial jargon you did not understand? (Or if it was a service you did not personally use . . . ?)

Information services

Our definition of these services is wide, and potentially includes not only libraries and information centres but records, photocopying, printing and graphics, as well as database management and web design and construction work.

Pay particular attention to definitions of the following:

- loan of stock items to defined users – how does this extend to electronic items, e.g. e-journal articles, and to the physical format of documents, e.g. in particular proprietary file formats such as Portable Document Format, or for use on particular machines, e.g. personal digital assistants?
- purchase, receipt and circulation of journals – how does the concept of circulation operate in the electronic network used by you and your customer groups?
- loans from other information centres – what restrictions may be placed on your users through technical or licensing constraints?
- literature searches – are searches to be limited to material available elec-

tronically (whether the indexes or the material itself)?

- document delivery – what constitutes a document, and what constitutes delivery? (For example, does the LIS need to be an intermediary, but if not, how can the e-document be accounted for or controlled?)

Computer-based information systems and databases

It is useful here to remind ourselves of the differences between some types of database.

Bibliographic databases contain records of information either held in the organization or in other collections. Bibliographic databases can be of several further types, depending on how much of the original item is included or extracted:

- indicative – a record that gives brief details of author, title, publisher, etc.
- informative – a record that gives fuller details and perhaps some keywords to more fully describe the document
- full record – this contains details as above but also an extensive abstract which may give enough details to help the user decide if they need the full document
- full-text document – in addition to the details of the source, the full content of the original article is included. Some databases of this type may be restricted to a particular organization or group, e.g. for internal reports: an SLA should highlight any restrictions, e.g. on the sharing of passwords to databases, file directories or individual e-documents.

Databanks contain numeric data or chemical formulae, etc.

Directory databases contain names, telephone and fax numbers, e-mail addresses, etc.

It would be well to include definitions of the services known by names such as Selective Current Awareness News Services (SCANS) or Current Awareness Services and Information Alerting Services (CASIAS), which give references to newly acquired documents and other information sources. If the update bulletins are to be distributed electronically, any relevant information about formats should be included in the definitions to ensure that there is a record of any network requirements.

Information technology and communications networks

It is essential for the managers of an EIS to know what technology base is available for the distribution of their service. In an organization such as a college, a school or a local authority this should be relatively simple, as the selection and management of the technology base is likely to be managed centrally – although where the customers are an external community, such as distance learners or residents of a local authority area seeking to use the library remotely, it is difficult to get answers to these vital questions.

In these cases, there could be competing pressures to go for a low common level for the computing platform, or to set high technological standards in the expectation that users would upgrade to that level to use the service. Either approach has its pitfalls. One the one hand, the use of older technology platforms offers quite unsophisticated service to users, while there is a risk of losing technical support as providers move to new technology. On the other, a move to the latest platform disadvantages users, especially those at the poorer end of the social scale, and excludes them from the higher levels of service enjoyed by the more affluent service users.

It is important to know what technology the users have, as without this information, it is possible that you may be providing information in unsuitable formats that customers cannot access or store.

The kind of question that can provide useful answers for developing an electronic information service would include:

- What telephone service can users access, especially in terms of storage and retrieval of fax documents, text messages and other graphic or character formats?
- Is there a network available to all members of the community? Does everyone know how to use it fully?

- Do users have access to common software tools, such as Microsoft Office or a compatible program suite? In dealing with corporate bodies, is the office automated system standalone on individual computers or is it linked to everyone?

Customer needs

The design of an EIS needs to take account of the needs of non-customers as well as existing users of the service. There is a range of customers and potential customers in many organizations, and it includes those who believe that they do not ever need to make use of external information sources (even if 'external' means the library in the next corridor). The LIS needs to demonstrate that information is vital to people in all kinds of organization and community.

In the context of the EIS, remember that – as has happened with the internet – the fact that information is available on the desktop using new information and communication technologies is likely to make the service attractive to those who previously made no use of it. At the same time, there is potential to lose those customers who are technophobes or fear that the EIS somehow reduces the personal quality of service. The achievement you are looking for is to attract sensible use from the first group while retaining the patronage of the second.

Let us suggest a categorization of customers:

- those who never use information
- those who are timid users, and typically wish to make greater use of the service but feel they are disrupting its operation by making use of it
- those who are sporadic users, and typically believe they have all the information they need, using the service only when their own resources fail
- those devoted information users who make full use of the services on offer and who act as champions of the LIS.

Each of these types requires a different approach, especially in the context of EIS. This is for two reasons. First, the positive and negative features associated with paper-based, 'traditional' LIS facilities by each of these types are likely to be replaced by other factors when faced with an electronic service. This means that planning a single approach to dealing with under-use of the LIS is likely to be too simplistic, and will fail to convey the range of services on offer. Second, people in the non-user, sporadic user and (to some extent) timid user categories may feel that they are experts on electronic information services, equating them directly with information technology or with their perception of the internet, and leading to possible misunderstandings. A careful and well-informed approach is needed here.

Information sources and non-users

Easy access to information repositories such as the world wide web make many people believe that a vast electronic library of reliable information is constantly at their fingertips. The information professional knows better, but it may be difficult to prove that mediated services are better than the sometimes hit-and-miss detail on offer through the web. This is a new-century version of the well-documented problem of the 1970s and 1980s, that of under-use of information services. It is important to stress that the web is no more infallible than colleagues and friends when it comes to supplying information on which major decisions, business or personal, are to be taken. Remind users that the information professional's training provides him or her with the skills to evaluate and filter information, and to be far more certain than untrained acquaintances of finding the correct information or assessing the risk of using a particular item of data.

When discussing their information needs, you need to press home the crucial question 'On what information do you depend to do your job?'

Your best approach to these questions is to adapt the matrices that we have produced for information audit work, seeking to identify the requirements that can be met through electronic services and mapping these on to the services offered by the electronic services available. You will need to have a form for each staff member or group you interview. A sample proforma is included earlier in this chapter (see page 24–5), but you can adapt it for your own use. There are also software packages that will support this work.

Further considerations in selecting the information sources with the greatest potential contribution to your service should include an assessment of the time requirements of the majority of users. Do your users require access to information quickly or immediately – the 'desperate' or 'urgent' categories of use – suggesting a need for access to electronic journals on the desktop, or the use of intermediated online services and the internet? Or are they able to wait longer, suggesting that if there is a price advantage they could be adequately served by traditional services?

Communication and marketing

The take-up of e-services will depend to some extent on the marketing and promotion that is used to support their launch. Many users will have only a vague idea of what is involved or how to access the range of services on offer. A marketing strategy is essential to support the investment in the new services and should explain how you will:

- inform your users about the services that you offer from the LIS or via electronic networks
- advise your customers about the other information sources you can access
- offer electronic information support to any new project
- make the new services visible to the potential user community.

The 24/7 e-information service

A major advantage of electronic services is that they can generally be made available 24 hours a day, seven days a week. Thought must be given to a number of issues in this situation, however.

User support – the 24-hour helpdesk

We showed in Chapter 1 how the library and computing functions have drawn closer to each other in many organizations and communities through the process known as convergence. In many academic libraries, particularly outside core daytime opening hours, technology queries are likely to be dealt with by a librarian, and basic reference enquiries by a technician. But even this process is unlikely to produce a round-the-clock presence, while many libraries now provide at least one area where 24-hour access is possible.

One novel approach is to arrange for another comparable organization in another time zone to provide the required support. E-mail offers an obvious way of handling queries, although the remote library must be prepared to treat the overseas users as equally important as its own customers – especially as their requirements are likely to be urgent in the middle of their night! Examples of this approach include a library in London which has reciprocal arrangements with another academic library in New Zealand; multinational companies where libraries communicate electronically so that urgent enquiries are passed from library to library throughout the day and can be worked on 24 hours a day if necessary; and in one agreement outlined at an Australian conference, a three-way support arrangement that connects libraries in New South Wales, Western Australia and New Zealand (Smith, 1999).

Security

One unfortunate opportunity offered by the 24-hour library is the unauthorized removal of equipment or parts of it (such as computer chips). Make certain that equipment is secured, and if the security guarding service in your area is not capable of guarding your investment ensure that cameras and other recording equipment are prominently displayed to deter would-be thieves. Fire regulations make it difficult to secure any area completely, but visible deterrence will stop opportunists. There is probably less defence against determined felons, so perhaps the best line is to leave older (but still efficient) equipment in a 24-hour computer room, keeping the best and newest kit in the area that is staffed during daytime.

Crashes and failures

The feeling of isolation when system crashes or power failures occur is not entirely reserved for the middle of the night. One of us recalls a seminar at which a public library web manager from a southern English county described the problems when systems failure struck his branch library on a busy Saturday morning, with no hope of anyone at County Hall being able to reset the server until the following Monday. Power failure will probably prevent any use of the system, and users will understand. Server crashes will be less obvious because the terminals will still work. Users may make matters worse by trying to restart the service or otherwise interfering with the terminals. A decision needs to be taken whether the server will be restarted at any time, day or night, and routines established – and recorded – that will restore service. Responsibility for restarting the system, if necessary by attendance at the business location, needs to be allocated (and probably compensated for by an out-of-hours allowance for being on call). Test the routine out by stopping the server at a pre-arranged time. Observe the result and learn from it, so that in an emergency the routine will be effective.

Back-ups

It is not very long since one major library mounted a catalogue on the world wide web that was taken off line for maintenance on Sundays (although unfortunately this fact was not obvious to users until they had submitted their entire search through the enquiry interface, which remained available at all times). Systems need backing up; everybody understands this. Make it clear what time this happens, and preferably schedule it at a time that inconveniences fewest people. Early Sunday morning may be a good time, and it can be arranged that this takes place automatically rather than having to make a disappointing end to somebody's Saturday night out.

Twenty-four-hour service means just that: especially where the library projects its service on to the world wide web, there should be an effective service for as many hours a week as possible.

Staff and their training

An essential element of any EIS is the staff. Building the team that can provide and manage a successful service will take time. In this section we look at ways to build this team and to put into practice the ideas we discuss in this book. You will also find suggestions in our book *Becoming a successful intrapreneur: a practical guide to creating an innovative information service* (Pantry and Griffiths, 1998).

There are certainly advantages to team working, apart from the simple issues of continuity of presence and cover. Complex work plans are carried out better by teams: they can cover a wider range of roles than the individual, they provide quality assurance for each, and they can ensure that goals are reached even when other important issues intervene. Team members feed off each others' ideas and develop typically more complex and successful solutions to problems than do individuals working alone. And teams can send stronger signals of commitment and involvement in the solution of organizational problems than individuals can do alone.

See also the section on training in Chapter 3.

Skills and knowledge

It would be as well to assume a high level of professional skill as a pre-requisite. After all, no matter how astute the management skills and however artful the political skills of the information manager, unless he or she can deliver the goods when results are needed against deadlines, there will not be a second chance to use them.

In his classic text from 1985, *Intrapreneuring*, Gifford Pinchot offers ten commandments for the intrapreneur (an entrepreneur working from within an organization). These give us a starting point in considering the skills that team members require. We are looking as much for a state of mind as for definable skills, and for an attitude to the task in hand as much as for detailed technical knowledge.

Pinchot's commandments suggest some useful characteristics for team

35

members, and some new ways of working. Team members should be willing to turn their hand to any task needed to bring success to an information project. It is no good trying to run a dynamic, go-getting service with people whose go-getting dynamism stops dead when their support staff are on leave, or who see some work as beneath or beyond them. Work with the best, and the best people are flexible.

Hard work is called for. One of the problems of developing innovative services is that the main service needs to be kept going while the development takes place so you will be looking for flexibility and versatility in team members as a minimum. They will need to be good with people. They will need to convince others – often the movers and shakers – of the value of information, and to do so in a persuasive way rather than a confrontational way. It is not a wise move to suggest that it was about time people realized that the information centre had the information all along – even though it did.

From this it may be apparent that we believe that your training programme for the EIS must include not just the obvious technical training, and the networking meetings and conferences that will keep staff up to date with developments. What makes the essential difference is more wide-ranging training in areas such as communications skills, team building and team working, leadership and negotiation.

Serious training and continuous professional development ensure that the staff are more than one step ahead of the customer. They are a vital part of creating a successful EIS. The information manager will need to ensure that the budgets cover all the training required.

Business planning

Developing an EIS is a serious enterprise and deserves a serious approach to its implementation. The techniques of business planning will provide you with several useful tools that will help to ensure success.

Budgets and costs

Budgeting for the EIS should be a major task of the information manager and the team. Savings can be made by entering into consortia buying. Subscription agents can nowadays provide a vast range of services; they too have had to develop to keep their customers. Chapter 6 discusses these issues in more detail.

Time planning

Time planning is another essential element of successful EIS management. It takes time to arrange subscriptions, licences and technical facilities. Tackle the process by using project management techniques. Various project management software programs can help; likewise look at a title in the Successful LIS Professional Series - *Making project management work for you*, by Liz MacLachlan, which will take you through the planning stage by stage.

Competitors

The world may well be your oyster, but there are many competitors to your services who will try to be an alternative source of your pearls of wisdom. No business plan can be considered complete unless it addresses these competing services. It should assess the impact on your business of these competitors and propose ways of dealing with the challenge. In the context of a plan to develop an EIS, competitors are likely to be organizations that attempt to sell their services direct to your users. Do not be blind to the fact that these electronic services market their services aggressively; you may find that a department or division in your organization has signed up to a service without your knowledge as a result of a direct approach or special offer.

But also do not forget that free information on the internet – particularly from a supplier that claims an exclusive edge – is a competitor. The model of information provision via the world wide web is gradually changing to a paid-for approach. If your users decide to take their information budget to a web-based service, your service could end up being marginalized.

Ensure that your plan identifies all such threats, and shows how they will be offset through marketing, the development of new services, or whatever means is appropriate in your environment.

Summary

This chapter has shown that developing an electronic information service has many similarities to the development of any other information service. The skills needed to design and create a service that meets the needs of the customer community or organization are those of information audit and the identification of client needs, with the library and information professional in the role of consultant for this work.

Customer need may well include 24-hour service, but this brings a number of new issues such as security and support into play. Staff are an important factor in developing the service; they should be selected carefully and trained well. Finally, you should develop a range of business-planning skills – all of which will be valuable in creating and managing these innovative services.

3

WHERE ARE THE CUSTOMERS?

In this chapter we look at the customers for e-information services:

- who they are and where they are located
- how they access information
- the level of intermediation they need
- keeping existing customers
- identifying new customers
- the role of the information professional in customer e-service
- what kind of training they will all need.

Who are the customers of e-services?

In one sense, the obvious answer to this question is that every existing customer of an existing information service is a customer for a complementary e-service. But the introduction of electronic services widens the scope of the customer base for any LIS. The information user is no longer obliged to visit the service to interact directly, for example by browsing the shelves or meeting the staff face to face. So in theory the customers of e-services could be anyone who has access to a computer or other electronic terminal with the right software to gain entry to the remote information system.

The traditional pattern of service has been based on separate services each with a target audience, often defined by membership of another group. Thus in a single city, a public library, university library and various special libraries may have co-existed for many years. Eligibility to use the services of each would be defined by referring to certain characteristics of the users, such as where they live or work (public library), where they are educated (school or university library), or where they work (special libraries). Although in some cases permission to use another library could be created through co-operative schemes like SINTO or HATRICS, generally eligibility and membership have been clearly defined and usually exclusive.

The arrival of electronic information services changes this. The internet allows potential users to identify materials in libraries across the world and to gain access to a large number of items online. Even where full service is not available outside a controlled group, it is common for all internet users to have access to some information such as the online public access catalogue (the OPAC).

Yet, frequently, the services offered are based on what information professionals think is happening rather than on any hard evidence about user habits – and there is very little hard evidence about users or their habits. Surveys suggest that many of them continue to use other sources, and that many of them persist in the belief that the internet contains the whole of human knowledge in a convenient box (Law, 1997; Griffiths, 1999).

Even more worryingly, those surveys that have been published suggest contradictory behaviour. A recent American study of e-service use at Princeton (Goodman, 2002) found that 'users in the sciences look for current journal articles online first', but a slightly older French survey of surveys (Muet, 1999) found that the use of electronic journals was regarded as supplementary to the use of printed originals. However the French study did find a distinct difference between the habits of students of natural and liberal sciences.

The customers for some e-services are very broadly defined. In fact the library and information profession knows rather little about the users of electronic information services, and who those users or customers are (Akeroyd, 2001; Pinfield, 2001).

for money – how does the user know that he or she has found the
nformation, or all the information?
ce – how does the information service demonstrate that best value
ng obtained from the system?

are long used to receiving enquiries by telephone and letter, and
g with customers beyond the physical building. The professional
nt of reference staff has ensured that the customer has received the
propriate material to meet the enquiry as interpreted from the
's request and the detail available. In this case the remote customer
d the opportunity to look at the available material and judge which
fact best suit the requirement.
library service changes this. Using e-services, customers can now
erials online, and select the most useful publications for their
But they can also by-pass professional intervention altogether, and
sk of failing to find all the available materials, perhaps because of
f their search strategies, or perhaps because their lack of subject
e did not alert them to the absence of particular documents. But,
ll see shortly, creative use of modern technology can start to
this problem.

customers identified?

sical library, authorized customers are identified by a physical token
cket or patron card. This is recognized by the staff and an agreed
rileges is offered to the patron in accordance with his or her
ip. This token also acts as an acceptance by the patron of the rules
ich the collection is managed, for example by agreeing to a
number of items to be borrowed at a time.
r in virtual libraries there is no such recognition mechanism.
n use the library without being seen or recognized by staff.

Customers can be the members of an organ
wherever they are located. In this case the L
difficulties raised by the conflict between the n
widely scattered, and the terms of licensing a

Customers can even be the citizens of an ɛ

- In Michigan, USA, the Access Michigan p
  a range of publications through library ser
  premises, and other public places with su
- In Iceland, an agreement reached in Nov
  citizens access to a range of journals w
  accessed the web. Under this agreemen
  view these journals from their personal
  access provided from library and other in

To a considerable extent, therefore, the cu
anyone within the LIS's target audience, an
communications can be established with tl
this, with many library catalogues available c
literally be anywhere in the world, and an
information service want to offer any kind c
the ability to eavesdrop on the services
audience?

These issues raise problems that we co

- Access – how does the system know tha
  user, and how does it control the use m
- Intermediation – how does the librari
  requirements of users when they do r
  centre?

There are further issues that we consider
some worrying conclusions about the bu

- Valu
  best
- Fina
  is be

Acces

Librarie
to deali
judgem
most ap
custome
has lack
items in

The e
view ma
purpose.
run the r
failures c
knowled
as we sh
overcom

How are

In the ph
such as a
set of pri
members
under wl
maximun

Howev
Patrons c

There is no way of ensuring that they comply with the regulations of the library or any particular restrictions that may apply to the document that they are using.

In many cases, library software will require the user to provide a password to gain authorized access to the service. By way of example, Leicester University Library Distance Learning Unit provides a range of remote services to its registered users. These are accessed over the internet by providing a recognized password to the software. Once this is accepted, users can use the library OPAC, and order books and other materials to be delivered. There is also an extensive range of electronic resources including guides to web resources.

Web technology can provide much of the security required, but the solution must allow for those customers who will not (or, on many corporate networks, cannot) comply with the library server's security requirements, such as the use of cookies or security routines activated through particular scripts such as JavaScript or ActiveX.

Intermediation

Remote customers are likely to by-pass the library where they have direct access to primary sources and believe, rightly or not, that they possess the skills to retrieve all the information relevant to an enquiry. Customers who visit the information centre expect to obtain support in the use not only of information but of the technology that presents it. Where the visit to the information centre is not because the product, such as a CD-ROM is physically unavailable beyond the campus, or cannot be networked, then the user is more likely to want technical support in the use of the product. Indeed, most library and information professionals would argue that to refuse such service would be a poor way of running things.

However the value of professional intermediation is actually raised by these changes. By eliminating low-level enquiries through web and other electronic services, the information service creates the space for higher-value intermediation and more complex research by information staff. But there is a danger that, unless it is highlighted, this enhanced intermediation will be undervalued by users and by managers of the overall function into which the LIS fits.

Steering users through the more complex enquiries and knowing when to switch to professional online services is an important task. Identifying and certifying the quality of electronic sources is essential, and some sort of 'red label' applied by the LIS to certify the quality of an e-source should be seen as a badge to be earned by internal services through their quality control processes, and a sign of high value when applied to an external service.

Keeping existing customers

E-services give libraries and information centres the chance to expand their clientele and improve their service to existing customers with relatively little effort. Service improvements are possible, for example by providing additional access to materials in demand by appropriate licensing of electronic copies rather than depending on single copies in a fixed geographic location such as a short-loan collection. Additional customers can be given access to the collection – which may mean that larger numbers of the target audience are attracted by wider access rather than that the target audience is widened, with the possible consequence of poorer service to existing users.

But there are difficulties. Often the customer has higher-quality technology on his or her desk and perceives the library to be technologically backward. Because of the need to maintain access to older products this impression may well be justified, and the information service must work around this to minimize technical barriers to customer service. One commentator reports the problems of a library user seeking an early English book from an online source. In order to access the text she was faced with choices that included sending the whole book to a printer (surely a nonsense in an e-library), downloading to her home computer over a domestic telephone line, or finding a computer in the library with a zip drive in order to store a copy of a file larger than the capacity of a floppy disk (Jantz, 2001). So keeping customers may be difficult: faced with this kind of choice, users may decide to by-pass the library altogether and use other routes to information. And although the cost of updating computers is now relatively low, if the old machines need to be kept for use with CD-ROMs and other less technically advanced products, a good business case must be made for the investment, and space must be found for the growing pool of computers of different vintages.

Some players in the information market have realized that here lie opportunities for them. They are developing business models that give end-users direct access to information that was previously only available in libraries. e-brary is one such supplier, allowing users to search its range of books and pamphlets, and purchase copies of sections (using the copy function of the web browser) for a few cents, or to print out a few pages. Access is through a user interface that alters the configuration of the browser and allows the user to unlock security settings on the documents displayed in return for the appropriate sum. Payment is from an account set up using a credit card, and although e-brary declares its support for the role of the librarian, users can find quantities of information without professional intermediation (**www.ebrary.com**). One clear attraction is the ability to purchase the right to use a small quantity of an item in the collection, and although this collection is as yet not particularly large, it has a number of items likely to be sought by students and others unwilling to commit to buying an entire book for the sake of a few pages or even a few lines.

There are choices to be made and librarians need to decide which services to concentrate upon. It may be reasonable for library users to use electronic services such as e-brary for simple retrieval tasks, and the information professionals would then most effectively concentrate on ensuring that existing customers continue to use the library for their more complex enquiries. It would be far better to spend some effort on dealing with perceived problems in the library service than to spend it on trying to compete with services that are run on commercial lines and will succeed or fail on that basis.

From the library viewpoint, it is worth observing that a single electronic version of a document available from an online vendor will not be sufficient for all the potential users of the library. Different editions of Shakespeare are needed by doctoral researchers and A-level students, and a single online edition is unlikely to fit all sizes. The library will use its energies best by explaining this to users and offering a range of alternatives. Bad alternatives include doing nothing as users move to inferior but technologically attractive services, and making adverse comments about the electronic offerings without considering why they might be attractive to current library users (and non-users). Patrons will be more likely to remain good users of a library service that is visibly dealing with the issues that make the electronic alternatives attractive.

Inducements to desert

A number of reasons have been identified that may make existing users more likely to rely on external electronic services, and some of them are entirely valid. Research shows, for example, that in many libraries the OPAC is difficult to use and the information that contains is frequently incomplete.

In one observed case, a noted scientist complained that he would need to travel to Michigan from Europe in order to view a French mathematical treatise from the early 1970s. In the event there were copies in several university libraries in Paris, but their OPACs were unable to provide the search facilities needed to locate the document (Jacquesson, 2000).

Paradoxically, the complexity of digital library interfaces in the library may make customers more likely to desert to a single but incomplete alternative.

Each supplier seems to have developed a separate and incompatible interface through which its own offering of journals is displayed. In many academic libraries the range of materials needed is so great that as many as 18 different interfaces are found (Akeroyd, 2001, and quoting Rusbridge 1998) by the time that all types of CD-ROM and online system are counted, along with the library catalogue. The growing use of the web interface is a solution and a further threat at the same time: while it delivers a more uniform and widely understood presentation of the information, it also makes it more difficult to tell where that information has come from and whether the source is internal (and authoritative) or external (and in need of verification).

In another study, this time in the USA, a librarian found that physicists were going to a local e-print repository for information rather than using the more comprehensive INSPEC service. But there was a sting in the tail: although the scientists were missing out on a considerable area of literature because they were only accessing what was present in the archive, it was found that they were getting far superior current awareness because of the time delay in indexing literature in the e-print archive (Quigley, 2000). One solution here would clearly be to improve current awareness while at the same time making the INSPEC service better known and more widely available.

This message is increasingly being heard. In the legal field, free legal resource aggregators are building websites that provide services that almost match the paid-for suppliers (Jatkevicius et al., 2000). An important question for the librarians in this field is how they will demonstrate to users that the advantage in using the library and its paid-for services remains sufficient for them to remain faithful.

Keeping customers: what works

The bottom line seems clear enough: you can keep existing customers when you expand your e-service, but it takes effort. A number of e-suppliers are on the side of the librarian, principally the periodicals agents or book jobbers who have developed e-services with the support of and through supporting the information profession; but a number of new style web-based suppliers have more commercial motives and do not form part of this shared tradition.

Above all, make it easy for the customer. (Ranganathan's dictum holds true – save the time of the reader.) Customers for your e-service are not using it to be impressed by the use of Z39.50, or the range of technical interfaces that have been built for different CD-ROMs. They come to you because they have a paper to write by the end of the week, or they need to fix their garden, or because they need to know the stock price of a potential acquisition.

This approach demands a new range of skills from library and information professionals, and we look at these in more detail later in this chapter.

Identifying new customers

As we saw above, the introduction of electronic library services opens up a potentially worldwide audience. Unless some form of access control is implemented, web-based services are available to any customer who chooses to go to that particular site. While this increase in audience could be welcome in some circumstances, it is worth taking a step back and considering the consequences before opening up e-services to the wider public.

User expectations may be difficult to manage when some of those users are located in an organization outside the library's parent body. In the special library sector, there may be questions of commercial sensitivity that would make it more difficult to provide external services. In the education sector, there are potential problems with licensing which may make it difficult to provide a service to users located outside the physical boundaries of the institution. The rules controlling local government finance may make it more difficult to provide services to people who do not live, study or work in the local authority area. But it is clear that there are growing expectations that library and information professionals will tackle these problems in the near future.

Taking on new customers may be a risky move if, in order to serve them, you have to reduce the quality of service to your existing customers. Nevertheless, the evidence suggests that you may need to find new customers to maintain a visible level of use that equates to present levels, because fewer people are likely to visit the physical collections of your library. One way of dealing with this could be to install comparatively sophisticated web monitoring software (such as Webtrends). This can provide information about the users of your web-based services that includes their identity and navigation patterns, showing you whether you have an important number of external users and whether they are seeking information that is significantly different from what your 'home' users look for.

If you are satisfied that taking on new customers is a sensible move, and that you cannot rely on logs of web-based activity to demonstrate sustained and increased levels of use of the library service, then you should seek those users. Web-based distribution will be a considerable benefit: you then do not need to worry about the compatibility of the technology, and can concentrate on the content of the service.

Service to external users does not have to consist solely, or indeed at all, of the supply of electronic documents taken from the library's collection. The technical facilities that are readily available allow services to external customers to be delivered by e-mail, telephone or streaming media. The standard Microsoft Office desktop has facilities that can enable real-time interaction between user and information professional, and indeed some libraries have begun to use this technology (Smith, 1999).

Call centre technology also has potential for remote customer service in e-libraries; many centres have the facility to talk to a website user through a site using a split screen that allows the operator to see what is on the user's screen. A call centre terminal in the library support section can be used to talk the user through a problem, or highlight a resource. Some use is already being made of these facilities in distance learning, for example the Partnership in Global Learning, a Latin American distance learning project which is funded by the Lucent Technology Foundation, the philanthropic arm of one of the major software providers in this field.

With the reduction in business travel, there is considerable commercial impetus to develop this type of software facility and it could be worth watching.

Licensing arrangements will dictate some of the potential content of the service, and you may be contractually prevented from offering some parts of the collection to external users. At the same time you will have to recognize those areas where your collection is seen as a leader in the field, and where there is thus an expectation that it might be made more widely available. Licensing conditions may also prevent you from selling the service, and there may also be copyright constraints. In the latter case these will vary from country to country, and it would be more than prudent to obtain legal advice if you are considering taking on customers from outside your own country and providing them with e-services. Make sure that your adviser is conversant with copyright and intellectual property, and, preferably, understands the international as well as the domestic issues raised.

The role of the information professional in customer e-service

With the introduction of e-services, new professional skills come into play. If you are the manager of an e-service, you will need to ensure that your staff have the necessary further abilities. It will be important that others (customers and non-LIS professional managers) are aware of the range of skills they now require, since it may appear that the work is being deskilled by the increased use of external information sources.

The Special Libraries Association (1996) *Competencies of special librarians in the 21st century* includes the statement:

> The special librarian is a technology application leader who works with other members of the information management team to design and evaluate systems for information access that meet user needs. Where required, the special librarian provides instruction and support so that end users can make optimal use of the information resources available to them. The special librarian is capable of working in the hybrid world of print and electronic media and providing the best mix of information resources in the most appropriate formats for the environment.

This seems an excellent summary and would be hard to better. In the context we have been discussing, information professionals are doing excellent but undervalued work such as

- evaluating services and certifying the quality of websites
- providing support and training for people using networked e-services

- continuing the higher-value paid-for reference and search services that are not replaced by the new offerings
- finding new resources for the network
- understanding the search process and the improved quality their intervention can provide
- adding metadata to site links and e-documents so that retrieval becomes easier and hits are more relevant
- making the e-services easier to use than the suppliers have done.

Training

This will not happen without adequate training for all involved. The field is moving rapidly, and the presence of a number of national and international projects ensures that there is a steady stream of reports and other experience to be shared.

For many practitioners the best training is likely to be in the form of participation at conferences and other exchanges of experience. The highly technical nature of some areas of the work highlights the need for specialist workshops as well as more general awareness sessions. Frontline support staff will need a different kind of training, to ensure that they can talk users through the service both for initial understanding and to resolve any later problems. Helpdesk skills will be important where few customers visit the library but rely on e-mail or telephone contact to resolve problems.

Many staff require wider skills than in the traditional library and this may need to be picked up in formal training programmes. As we note in the section on convergence, technical staff need to acquire basic library skills including simple enquiry work, while librarians need to have basic technical skills that will allow service to continue out of standard working hours.

As we saw above, many users of the service will need to understand the changes that have taken place in the service. Areas such as copyright and intellectual property will need particular attention, as it is here that problems can unintentionally arise. Even where, as with the recent changes in Australian copyright law, the onus is on the external user to comply with the law rather more than it is on the library providing the service, it is vital that users understand their obligations and do not inadvertently fall foul of the rules.

A training statement should form part of the plan for introducing electronic information services. It should cover staff, users and the management structure within which the information and library service is located. It may be appropriate to include presentations to the board of directors, academic board or council of your organization in this statement. The statement will cover library and information professional, technical and communications training, and include details of any training of trainers that may be required, for example in preparation for a cascaded introduction of the e-service. Do not underestimate the resources needed for this work, either in terms of the cost of training, or (as has emerged from the introduction of the People's Network in the UK's public libraries) to cover the essential work of those being trained.

See also the section on staff training in Chapter 2.

Summary

At the outset it may have appeared obvious who the customers would be for e-services, but this has been shown not to be so. Although the answer will vary for every service for a variety of political and commercial reasons, it is essential to identify the target audience and decide who is a legitimate user of the service.

You should now have a checklist of issues to be resolved around the identity and location of customers, as well as a note of any concerns about the current business and its users, who may be a different group from the e-service clients. Your list will cover the ways in which new customers can be attracted and served, and a note of the skills that your staff will need to support this activity.

4

WHAT KIND OF INFORMATION DO YOUR CUSTOMERS NEED?

In this chapter we look at the types of information that your customers need and the formats that it can be supplied in. We look at:

*   what your information audit tells you
*   types of information:
    *   general information
    *   scientific, technical or medical information
    *   business and financial information
    *   legal information
    *   educational information
*   how often customers need this information
*   the formats in which the information can be presented
*   other considerations
*   new partnerships
*   turning information into a value-added service.

What your information audit tells you

In Chapter 2 we saw how important the information audit is. Information managers need a clear understanding of the entire organization or community in which the service will operate, as without that understanding the information service will not achieve a central role in the user community.

Irrespective of the subject background, the organization's or the community's needs should be identified and captured before work begins on the design and creation of the service, or the identification of the electronic components within it. We saw that this audit would tell the manager:

- what information exists within the organization
- where it is located
- what information the organization needs and when it is needed
- who uses it
- what gaps exist
- where potential customers for information are in the organization
- why people use a particular service or source of information in preference to others
- why some people use the service frequently or occasionally
- why some people never use the service
- how to produce the information in the format needed.

To this list we can add:

- where the customers are located within the organization (either geographically or organizationally)
- who needs the information
- what information they need and when.

There are many opportunities to develop new services that may not fit into the traditional mainstream of library and information work but call upon the skills of the information professional. In many countries a range of initiatives is now being developed at national level that is founded on the creative use of information. Information professionals are presented with a range of publicly backed projects that will benefit from trained professional input.

General information

No doubt while you were carrying out your information audit you established just how much general information is needed across the whole of the organization. Fortunately, over the past few years many directories, encyclopedias, handbooks and other general reference works have become accessible electronically, either on disc or over the internet. This makes it easy for the EIS to make contractual agreements for access and offer these services to the end-user customer. Many of these services are free of charge and can be offered on the intranet to your customers where your customers are allowed direct internet access from the desktop. We are aware that in many organizations, either for policy or other reasons such as the configuration of the firewalls, most employees are denied access to internet-based services. In these instances you should still be able to offer a service, either using standalone computers in the LIS and elsewhere or, where controls are very tight, as an intermediated service from the library.

Here are some possible services that can be provided electronically in the field of general and reference information:

- links to postcode and address finders
- timetables – rail, bus and air
- maps, including country, town and Ordnance Survey maps
- government departments and agencies
- European Commission information services and publications
- newspapers
- acronyms and abbreviations listings
- dictionaries
- encyclopedias
- information handbooks
- university prospectuses and handbooks
- national collections.

Digital reference

Only a few years ago, the term 'digital reference' would have been unknown, but today it is the mainstay of many electronic and networked services. This is an area where your EIS can really score. People are now using the internet as an everyday tool to find answers to reference questions. This offers an opportunity for the information professional to provide a remote reference service to users both within and outside the organization or community, providing links to high-quality search services or to reference sites in specialist subjects via an intranet or extranet, or through an internet website accessible to all members of the community (which can be password protected if necessary).

'It is all there on the internet and it's free' is a widely held view that tends to provoke cynical laughter from information professionals. In the USA, for example, digital reference can no longer be considered as simply the future model of information services – it has arrived and is likely to become a mainstay of electronic and networked services (Lankes et al., 2000). As just one example, the Virtual Reference Desk Project (**www.vrd.org**) has been a pioneer in digital reference and one of the foremost efforts to better understand and use digital reference for the networked environment.

Standards

The EIS can set standards for a quality information service through the quality of the links that it selects and makes available.

Users of electronic services until the mid-1990s were used to searching online databases using command languages that were often difficult to structure for complex queries. Much library computing was done on mainframes and tasks such as obtaining a printout of budget spending involved knowledge of command language since there was no user-friendly interface. Microcomputers were often used as dial-up terminals to interrogate online databases. Standards were relatively unimportant to the LIS user, although of course they had long existed in areas such as cataloguing and indexing.

The arrival of the world wide web in the mid-1990s set a common standard for the first time that affected many average computer users. The protocols adopted for delivery of information from the web have developed but are still recognizably the same as those first adopted to present pages of information through the Mosaic browser, and hyperlinking to other pages.

Since then a number of standards have emerged for document delivery. Microsoft standards, particularly the Word .doc format, have become an important means by which much information is presented. However these formats are increasingly liable to conceal a virus; and they are open to the possibility of alteration. They are also a poor method of presenting the original layout of the document (for example, if the reader does not have the original font installed), but not as poor in this respect as Hypertext Markup Language (HTML) which is frequently encountered as a format for document delivery.

The proprietary standard Portable Document Format (.pdf) is widely used where layout and appearance are important. Using Adobe Acrobat or another program capable of outputting documents in this format, the author can ensure that the layout of the document is preserved and can regulate the user's ability to copy or amend the text. However the user of .pdf files must have the Acrobat reader installed: this is a large download, and although the program is not complex to install and free of charge this technical process remains a barrier to use for the technically less able user. In a community where a central resource manages information technology, this is not a problem, but a public library service needs to consider how it might offer technical guidance to users of its services beyond the library walls.

The use of web standards has provided a common platform for computer-based library services. They have been joined by recognized technical standards such as Z39.50 (ISO 23950) that allow systems to transfer information and communicate with one another (Miller, 1999).

Then there are other standards where library and information professional skills are in demand, notably the application of metadata. Metadata, often defined as 'data about data', helps to describe documents using standard fields. In the scheme known as the Dublin Core, there are 15 standard fields that many LIS professionals will recognize as elements of bibliographic description.

Round-the-clock service

This standards-based approach opens the opportunity for the notion of the 24/7 (24 hours a day, seven days a week) digital reference service, available on a website or network even out of service hours, when the LIS is closed.

This notion of 24/7 digital reference services opens new doors for innovative services. Very importantly, it also offers information professionals new opportunities to set standards for quality information services in the provision of remote reference services. The emergence of a digital and distributed information environment has temporarily unbalanced a relationship that has been stable for the past hundred years or so, but reference specialists are not about to become extinct or an endangered species. By identifying the users' new kinds of information seeking behaviour, they can forge new kinds of relationship with users, taking the opportunities afforded by information and communication technologies to develop a new kind of reference service culture.

The information professional should easily be able to establish the information requirements of LIS customers in terms of databases, subject categories, and other sources such as news feeds. These sources can then be 'pushed' to their customers using the kind of technology that Amazon.com has already demonstrated will work in a commercial model. The result is a stream of relevant information to the customer that the information professional observes and adjusts in line with the user's comments and the development of the subject area – for example when new terminology enters common use and needs to be added to the search profile.

Scientific, technical or medical (STM) information

A recent study shows that 72% of the 4.2 million articles requested annually from the British libraries are for scientific technical or medical materials –

by far the largest proportion for any subject. Many respondents to a survey carried out by the Ingenta Institute reported that they made regular orders for articles in electronic format. Suppliers fall into two broad categories: those which make a flat charge and then allow unlimited access, and those which allow free searching but charge for each article displayed or printed out. Research suggests that while subscription services are probably better suited to library use, many scientists make use of the pay-per-article services because they have authority to spend small amounts of money or even because they are willing to pay for the low prices from their own pockets.

However this entirely changes the traditional economics of general production in the STM field. Access becomes as important as possession of the materials, and some of the major scientific publishers have also become the direct sellers of information to the end-user. Many of the new information retailers provide web-based additional services such as discussion groups. The researcher's choice of service may be dictated in the end as much by the appearance and facilities of a particular website as by the quality of the information that appears there.

So, depending on the subject areas you need to cover, there is a wealth of databases, both full text and bibliographic, available in the STM field. To find the most suitable services, evaluate candidate suppliers with your customers. Most e-suppliers will arrange free trial subscriptions so you, the EIS staff and customers can evaluate the contents of the services against their everyday needs.

This is the field in which many of the major suppliers have their most extensive catalogues. They include Ovid Technologies/SilverPlatter Information Services, SwetsBlackwell, Dialog, the European Commission, US National Library of Medicine, and standards associations – but there are many more specialist electronic publishers and suppliers besides. Do not forget the health, safety, fire, chemical and environmental information that all organizations need, irrespective of their size, to be able to meet their legal obligations.

You need to decide on the journals, conference and other papers, standards, legislation, and other information that you wish to access. Draw up a list of criteria against which you can evaluate each potential service for the EIS, e.g.:

- Is the service easy and intuitive to use by both EIS staff and customers?
- Will much training be needed?
- Is the content comprehensive for your needs? Or will you have to arrange for another service to cover the gaps?
- How far back in time does the information cover? (And is there a gap before the service begins, forcing you to store long runs of paper copies?)
- Will the EIS continue to allow access to the data for the period of your subscription should you decide to cancel some time in the future?
- Are there clauses in the agreement that restrict your rights?
- Are there any other restrictions such as the available times for access? (It is no use you trying to provide a 24/7 service to find that the service you want is only available 90% of time.)

Business and financial information

Users of business and financial information are already used to an environment where information purchased at a high price can be useless 20 minutes after its original delivery. In many cases, the availability of electronic copies of journal articles and books is of secondary importance since much of the information used for decision making is taken from real-time databases. The cost of the most valuable services is likely to be high, although limited services are available on the world wide web. For example, the *Economist* website makes a proportion of the week's published content available free of charge to all users. This site is also one of many that provide subscribers to the printed version of the newspaper with access to additional content, giving them electronic access to the full range of articles.

Business information is in fact poorly suited to the way that many electronic journal publishers operate, and most value is likely to come from newspapers, weekly publications, and broadcast media websites. Because many publishers impose a one-to two-year moratorium before they place a journal in a full-text electronic library, the text of many business and financial journals is not easily available other than in printed form during the period in which it is the most use for research. It is much easier to find suitable materials for historical studies in this field. For current research, sources such as conventional paid-for online databases are of more use than electronic journal repositories. For current information on stock prices there may be no alternative to expensive online services; information only becomes free when it is of no immediate value. However, e-suppliers may be able to offer you an amalgamation of services, or a basket of individual features matching the needs of your customers.

There are many competing business news and financial information services, each claiming that they have the best coverage. It is finally up to you and your customers to decide what is required to meet your particular everyday needs.

Typical suppliers whose services you might consider include:

- Bureau van Dijk, whose range includes regionally tailored databases covering either geographic areas (the UK, Europe or worldwide) or information by sector (insurance and banking)
- Business Monitor International, whose services cover emerging markets and risk evaluation
- Croner.CCH, which covers a range of market sectors in the UK, and has five web centres which provide access to information for some of these sectors
- Hemscott, which provides a range of company research products online
- Lexis/Nexis, who have moved from their original offering of primarily legal and general news services to providing information services to support decision making in business.

These are just some of a far wider range of UK-based and other services. In France, for example, such databases are so well established as consumer products that television advertisements regularly promote the company information service Euridile during breakfast programmes and evening news bulletins when business decision makers (and their support staff!) are likely to be watching.

Long-standing reference tools such as the Kompass directories are also available in electronic format, as are financial newspapers such as the *Financial Times* and the *Economist* (whose website we mentioned above). A further range of providers offers differing approaches to current business news; these providers include names such as the BBC and Reuters, as well as newer arrivals such as Bloomberg.

Legal information

Many organizations rely heavily on legal information. Not only do solicitors and legal firms require extensive access to electronic legal information, but so do government departments and agencies, law faculties and other departments of universities, and many company departments such as human resources, health and safety, and international divisions. Legal information is very complicated, and constantly changing: for example, there were over 4000 separate pieces of legislation covering the UK in 2001, not to mention those unique to Scotland, Northern Ireland and Wales. Your customers must also be alerted to a stream of Directives, Recommendations and Decisions coming from the European Parliament and Council that will eventually find their way on to the statute book of each member state. Add to this the steady flow of case law and law reports and a complex picture emerges.

A number of electronic services are well established in this field. Butterworths provide access to a number of services including Halsbury's Laws and the All England services as well as to case search, legislation and training and contracts material. Other suppliers include Lawtel, Smith Bernal, Context, Sweet and Maxwell, and Westlaw.

Commentary is also available from a number of legal firms who provide libraries of opinion and comment on the web. While many LIS state clearly that they (quite rightly) do not offer legal opinions as part of the service, and while these commentaries also carry similar health warnings, the websites of legal firms are a useful reference resource in highlighting the issues around particular topics. Your organization or community should insist, however, that a qualified legal practitioner should rule on any decisions made using such information before any action is taken as a result.

Educational information

Bill Gates, the CEO of Microsoft Corporation, wrote to the Australian Library and Information Association before Australian Library Week 1998, that his involvement with and support of libraries in the USA was 'to ensure that people of all communities have access to the Internet. I see it as a great opportunity to reach out and have the world at their fingertips, to seek out and share information and to learn throughout their lives.'

In the UK, the then Heritage Secretary, Chris Smith MP, launched National Library Week 1997 by describing public libraries as 'the universities for ordinary people, [providing] access to new communications technology for thousands of people who can not do so at home'.

There are many examples, but it is the EIS and the skill of its staff that can help all staff in the organization to continuously update their skills and knowledge. As an extension of this, the EIS can use new technology to support its programmes. Imaginative use of technology can improve access for many groups of people, especially where these groups have special needs because of disability, remote location or other factors that have precluded their access to library and information services.

The education sector has also produced some innovative uses of information technology, such as the UK's National Grid for Learning (NGfL), providing access to a wide range of resources to support life-long learning. Also in the UK, the New Opportunities Fund is funding the roll-out of an extensive programme of publicly accessible centres under the UK online banner, of which around 4300 will be in public libraries, and others in colleges and other locations where LIS professionals are employed and can expect to play an important role in providing the public with access to electronic information services.

How often will the customers need this information?

An information audit will provide the EIS with information about the frequency of updates that customers need in their particular subject areas, and also the maximum acceptable delay in supplying information. The service level agreement (SLA), which we discussed earlier in the book, will act as an agreed record of the speed and timeliness of updates that your customers have accepted.

Differences between sectors in which LIS professionals work are likely to be particularly marked over this question. In the academic sector, there will be fluctuations during the academic year and for some of the reasons we discuss above the availability of information in electronic format will happen much later than for some other sectors, such as the financial and business areas. In areas such as medical and scientific research, updates are likely to be required quickly from journals carrying important research results; while in local and central government, news and other current information is required more and more quickly. Government also has a growing need for access to local news services, so that frequently updated local newspaper websites are of increasing value.

Formats for presenting electronic information: constraints and innovative services

It would be easy to devote this entire book to the ways in which new technology and information professionals – people perceived as being very traditional – have become great enthusiasts for new technology. It comes as a surprise to many to realize that, two decades ago, the precursors of today's fast Pentium PCs were chunky electric typewriters with acoustic couplers built in, working at only one-hundredth of the transfer rates now standard. But even then libraries were using these to access news and database services, and impressing their customers with what was then an amazing technological advance as these 'dumb' terminals typed their message at a blistering rate of 30 characters a second.

To ensure that the EIS provides rapid and well-informed access to (and guidance on) electronic services, it is important that the staff is fully aware of the range of opportunities.

The introduction of computer-based services can produce problems at the working level. You may find yourself having to take apparently trivial decisions to keep services working. And you will find that other services have taken opposing decisions in the same situation!

Typical of this kind of issue might be deciding the numbers and availability of public access terminals, and how they should be used. Some users occupy computers in libraries, particularly public libraries, for long periods and effectively block other patrons from using your electronic services. How do you deal with this?

- 'Children can never get onto the computers to do their homework because the adults have got to them first,' according to Michael Hill, an expert in the management of complaints. 'In Camden, they have set up a 4pm to 5pm slot when children have priority as a result of youngsters' complaints' (Vandevelde, 2002).
- The Grand-Fort Philippe Library (located in a small commune on the north French coast near Dunkerque) decided to remove CD-ROMs from the intranet network in order to make best use of the limited number of terminals. It was feared that children would occupy the terminals for long periods to use the CD-ROMs and thus prevent other research using the intranet and its web connections (Deconinck and Gauchet, 1998).

The Gates Foundation commissioned a survey in 2000 that found a similar pattern. The problems of demand and lack of access were raised, but also the immense value of public access to computers in the libraries surveyed. The study found evidence that public access computers were drawing their users to the library more frequently than other types of library visitor and that they stayed longer on each visit. Although there was less demand from those having computer access at home, these people showed the same characteristics of use. Although most people used the library computers for managing their borrowing and finding things in the catalogue, almost as many used the computers for internet access. As well as making a demand for more machines to be available, users commented on the need for training in their use, the need for more publicity to tell patrons the machines were there – and the fact that noise levels tended to be higher in libraries where they were installed. One person commented, 'When I want to read, [now] I go to a coffee shop' (Gordon, Gordon and Moore, 2001).

So the opportunity is there for the EIS to address these issues by really acting as an access centre, to allow as many people as possible to use computers and online information services. Speakers of minority languages can be better served by access to information in their language even when staff who speak it are absent.

Case Study A

Queens Library in New York has 'Las Paginas en Español', which allows the 20% of its population whose first language is Spanish to search the library's catalogue in that language. It also runs programmes to develop Russian and Turkish collections in areas with high immigrant populations. It also provides a multilingual interface to the internet, WorldLinQ, developed at the Library, which allows Chinese, Korean and other non-Roman characters to be displayed on a computer screen. Daily newspapers from China, Taiwan and Korea can be read on the internet, and Chinese libraries accessed from Queens.

Case Study B

In the western isles of Scotland, the Gateway Project has been successfully submitted to the Scottish Office Public Libraries Challenge Fund by Comhairle nan Eilean Siar (formerly the Western Isles Council) which seeks to generate interest and support for the Gaelic language, and to foster community identity with reference to culture and oral tradition. Coventry Libraries has produced a CD-ROM as a project with the local Irish community that will include the experiences of the community in the UK, its culture, literature and language.

But it is not only members of minority-language-speaking groups who can benefit from libraries' imaginative use of technology. Rural communities are disadvantaged by their location, at least so far as access to libraries is concerned. Australia provides many examples. In the Northern Territory, community libraries are typically surrounded by cattle stations or wetlands with crocodiles or fish. Yet through links with educational facilities they offer technology-based modern services to a seasonal demand that turns on the timing of the rains and school terms. In another part of the Territory, the Yulara community library at Uluru (formerly Ayer's Rock) combines resources such as storytelling relating to the Aboriginal people's sacred site with internet access. In Queensland public libraries are described as 'the people's on-ramps to the Information Superhighway' despite the 'vast spaces and tyrannical distances' of that state.

Another example of the use of technology to deliver information to customers at various levels is the MAD Scientist Network (**www.madsci.org**) which is a web-based ask-a-scientist service with some years' experience now in handling questions from the public. It is a volunteer organization of over 800 scientists from around the world who answer a wide range of scientific questions at all levels. They have developed an archive of questions and have neatly classified the scientific groups, e.g. from astronomy to physics. This helps them to answer a large volume of questions and also they have developed software to help process the questions, to allow the service to effectively respond to the majority of questions received.

Other groups who benefit from innovative use of new technology by libraries include senior citizens. Baltimore County Public Library Senior Center provides an internet page containing links to resources for senior citizens. Librarians gather information from a range of sources, including directories and flyers, and enter it on a database reached by hyperlinks from the page. And the electronic information is increasingly accessible to the partially sighted, either by the ability of the computer to increase the font size viewed on the screen, or by software which reads aloud text pasted to the Windows clipboard. Senior citizens may well be able to contribute in return to local history collections. Many suburban areas now have few of their original residents remaining and their early history is close to being lost.

Although children are frequently thought of as more technically literate than the rest of the population, they still have some special needs in library services. Besides the range of services we described in the case studies above, Queens Library in New York runs a special programme for teenage parents together with their babies and their own parents, to demonstrate the use of library services for support in parenting and for continuing their education. Children's computer literacy can help to deliver their needs and UKOLN's Treasure Island internet pages (**www.ukoln.ac.uk/services/ treasure/**) are another approach to this.

The library can use the new technology as a means of processing its collections and as a means of publishing in novel forms, and use the new technology to enhance access to its collections

The price of CD-ROM publishing is now lower than conventional print on paper for many applications. For projects such as the Coventry Libraries CD-ROM, its cost-effectiveness is enhanced by its ability to store a range of formats including sound and images. Another of the successful Scottish Office Public Library Challenge projects is The Virtual Mitchell: this includes plans to digitize materials from the riches of Glasgow's Mitchell Library and its City Archives, and to make these searchable and available over the City Council's network and on the internet (**www.mitchelllibrary.org/vm/**).

Life-long learning and library services

Life-long learning has been around for far longer than the name which is now applied to it, and libraries have been part of that process for a hundred years or more. Their role in life-long education provides scope for further innovative services. The UK Government's Green Paper *The Learning Age* notes that the public library service holds an enormous range of educational material and has the potential to deliver information and learning to people of all ages and backgrounds, right across the country. 'The Learning Age,' says the report, 'will be supported by the development of new information and communication technology within libraries.' Proposals are to be produced for a public libraries IT network as an integral part of the National Grid for Learning.

But this role is not only one for public libraries. Others following the principles of Investors in People should consider the role of their library or information centres as open learning centres to support training and development. The use of multimedia technology fits well with the modern corporate library – or indeed the academic library – but the traditional printed book and periodical continue to have a strong claim to a place in this environment.

Acting as guide and coach

The rapid growth of technology leaves many people in need of help, support or explanation. Many people in the UK have taken advantage of the series of schemes promoted by the Government and others such as the BBC making use of public libraries to introduce new technology to ordinary users. Under the titles 'Computers Don't Bite' and later 'Webwise', many people were given a 'test drive' designed for new users of computers. The UK online centres will continue this theme.

More generally, libraries are in an ideal position to act as guide and coach to those unfamiliar with new technology. Libraries have long been users of technology. Now the early computerized catalogues of the late 1960s have given way to widespread use of PC networks and the internet. The librarian's (largely unappreciated) technical knowledge is at last being matched by some reported development of library skills among IT staff.

This traditional role of the library may well be an appropriate one to develop in an intrapreneurial role. In the corporate or academic environment, the information or learning centre provides a central outlet for mentoring and support services which aligns perfectly with its role as the central information resource.

Computer-assisted learning and other services are starting to appear in the more progressive public libraries. In a number of government agencies, the development of open learning facilities has been followed by close working between the library and training sections in recognition of the overlap of interest. In both public and private sector organizations, the installation of extensive IT networks has been accompanied by minimal training: there are constant reports of the banal level of many enquiries to support staff. (How do I print the page? How do I get the sticky label out of the printer roller so it works properly again?)

There are, of course, issues of training and development for information and library professionals and support staff. Their initial training provides many of the skills needed to deal with the coaching role, but time and resource needs to be devoted to developing familiarity with new software and other facilities. If new services are to be offered, the library service must be confident in its ability to provide, and its users must be confident in the librarians' skills.

Other considerations

Keep in mind the possibility of the emergence of practical problems in developing the EIS. The *New Library* report (LIC, 1997) points at a number of related issues that, again, are not solely questions for the public library service. For example, longer opening hours are necessary if services are to be provided at times to suit potential users. University libraries are experimenting with 24-hour opening, allowing students approaching finals to make use of the (often unattended) service at any time of day or night. Public libraries experimented with all-night opening during 1997 National Library Week, with some success. Special EIS in locations such as hospitals provide access at all hours, although in all these instances, professional service at unusual hours is the exception (media EIS, for instance) rather than the rule – or even the hint of a rule. Yet with more part-time working and home working, and individuals increasingly holding more than one part-time job, the question of EIS opening hours is clearly important, and finding innovative ways of extending service within existing budgets is a priority.

In business, this encompasses many changes. There are many technical questions such as the use of information in corporate change. Education is no longer simply a matter of schooling, even though professionally-run school library services are a fairly recent innovation in many areas. The development of life-long learning and support for civic education are two examples of new and information-hungry forms of education far removed from the traditional school curriculum.

Likewise when creating the EIS you need to be aware of the intellectual property rights in the context of the digital information service: for example, who owns the answers to enquiries? and what is the concept of fair use? Care is needed when setting up such services so that everyone involved understands the implications.

New partnerships

Partnerships between publicly funded libraries and the private sector, while largely taboo even 20 years ago, are now acceptable and offer opportunities for appropriate development of new services. There was at one time caution about using any materials with commercial connections, but in the current climate sponsorship is proving a valuable way of developing new services. In another form of sponsorship, the longer opening hours and Sunday opening as an innovative service are being underwritten in some places by local sponsors.

Turning information into a value-added service

Information is a commodity whose value is finally being understood and appreciated. Manufacturers and vendors of intelligent agent software promote their products on the basis that the discovery, storage, management and retrieval of information is a complex process whose value warrants their investment. The information profession adds value to information in every sector, and interprets or retrieves it for the benefit of customers. That is truly what the EIS is about.

Summary

In this chapter we have seen:

- many examples of innovative services
- a wide range of approaches to the development of innovative services (interestingly, although we could have quoted extensively from examples taken from special libraries, almost all our examples are from the public and academic library and information sectors)
- a common approach to information which adds value to it, either by its being appropriate for its particular audience, or by bringing together items which are otherwise separate
- how to build on the traditional strengths of the library service to provide a modern EIS
- why the EIS looks for the opportunities to develop new value from existing resources, or new resources to develop further value.

5

WHO NEEDS TO BE INVOLVED IN YOUR PLANS?

In this chapter we look at who needs to be involved in your plans:

- internal interests
  - staff
  - other departments of the organization
  - internal contractors and suppliers
- external interests
  - external suppliers
  - external customers.

There are a number of interested parties apart from your customers and potential customers as you develop your EIS. Other internal and external players will have expectations and concerns that need to be addressed as part of your management and communications plans for the new service.

Because the nature of EIS is so radically different from what has gone before, it is important that you carry all interested parties with you. They need to understand what the service consists of, and their role in delivering and maintaining it. They need the confidence to use the service successfully, and to understand any charging mechanisms that are associated with it.

Staff

If this is important for the customers or users of the service, it is doubly so for LIS staff. They are the people who will have to deliver the service and help users to understand what it contains, so they must have thorough training that will give them the necessary confidence to deal with enquiries and problems.

The initial stage is to ensure that LIS staff are in the picture from the development phase. They need to hear what is being planned and to receive regular bulletins on progress (or, probably, the lack of it for long periods of time). Take time to consider the means that can be used to provide information to the staff, and which are the most appropriate in your LIS.

Keeping your staff informed

Paper-based bulletins may be the most reassuring way to issue information. Many LIS have someone who is adept at producing bulletins using word-processing or desktop publishing software, but there are disadvantages. The concept of an EIS may be difficult to get across in simple text; and a paper bulletin seems a strange way to announce a change to digital media. Most of all, a paper bulletin gives the impression that discussion and decision making is complete and that no input is required from or available to the general staff of the LIS.

So a meeting may offer a better way of announcing what is to happen. (Or in an LIS context, meetings – plural – may be required if service is to be maintained: in this case, run them end to end, to avoid the members of the first meeting having time to give wrong ideas to the second group, based on any misunderstandings). A presentation (with some screen dumps of real EIS, if available) will help people to understand the concept. A copy of the presentation will make sure that the message is retained and allow your preferred terminology to get into circulation.

Time for questions will be essential, with someone standing by who is able to answer in layperson's terms where some of the more complex ideas are explained. Anticipate the obvious questions: Are we getting rid of the journals collection? Will people still come to the library to make enquiries? Is this a way of getting rid of library staff? Will I have to learn new skills or lose my job? Will you provide full training? Remember that change is an unsettling experience, even if you are keeping the traditional collection in full while the EIS is built up.

As well as the personal concerns that staff might express in the questions above, be ready for some of the more obvious technical and financial questions. Will the library catalogue need to be changed to manage hyperlinks to electronic journal articles? Is the campus or office network configured to allow the facilities the LIS needs (or has the LIS got to find some money for reconfiguration work?) And will this cost more, and reduce the funds for other activities?

Intranet sites are widely used to provide information about new projects, and for an EIS there is the added attraction that a website uses the same new technology that will carry the electronic publications. This makes it possible to create a small demonstration model, using some of the free content that is available on the world wide web to show how some forms of searching would work. You will probably want to protect this site with a password (issued to LIS staff) for the initial stages, to avoid wider discovery of this site until your own staff are familiar with its content. Include contact names that staff can call for further information, or provide an e-mailbox or a discussion group on the site.

The impression of progress in creating the EIS will be fostered if the site visibly changes in some way through regular updates, even if these are relatively small alterations. Amending the date on a static page shows that it has been visited by the author and declared current at a recent time, but a page left untouched and apparently unvisited for months is viewed as unreliable.

Smaller versions of some of the public awareness sessions suggested below may be worth organizing for LIS staff. Your suppliers may well already know several of the staff and a visit by their e-services manager to explain what is on offer may be enlightening for all concerned.

Staff representatives

Finally, do not forget to involve staff representatives in the process. Trades unions or staff associations will wish to be reassured that the interests of staff are being considered – although they will probably be reassured by the overall improvement in job quality that will result. And although there may be a reduction in the amount of routine processing that takes place (such as copying), there is likely to be an increase in higher-quality work such as dealing with intellectual property rights that at least compensates for these reductions.

Other parts of your organization

Once your staff are comfortable with the idea of an EIS and understand it well enough to describe it to others, you should let them help you to present the idea to other parts of the organization. Particularly if introducing the EIS involves changes to the existing service, users must be given good notice, and opportunities provided to feed back their comments on the proposals.

Much of the material that was developed for LIS staff will be useful for presenting the proposals to the organization at large. It may need to be edited for LIS jargon, but if it has been developed for all levels of LIS staff it will, we hope, be readily understood by most people.

Take time to look at other ways that the idea of the service can be explained to the rest of your organization, users or not.

Demonstration sessions

Demonstration sessions in the LIS can show bookmarked sites that offer free electronic content. Many web users are not used to looking for or evaluating serious content, so this could be very enlightening for them. We have mentioned several times that a section of the user base believes that every known fact (and then some) is on the web, and that mediated service is no longer needed. Demonstration sessions can demonstrate the falsity of this idea, perhaps by showing just how much bad and conflicting detail can be found. Demonstrations can also show users the quality of content that they cannot access but which is available to the LIS on subscription.

Videos

Does your organization have any kind of video presentation opportunities? (This might be streaming video on an intranet, or simply a television screen hooked on to a video recorder and placed in a public area such as a canteen.) Some of the videos produced by electronic information suppliers may appear corny but they are still a powerful tool. If there are suitable facilities, a short video could be produced in-house: perhaps the training department has suitable equipment for recording, or in an academic environment a media studies or communications course might develop a short video as a student project. But show the result to someone outside the project before it goes to a real audience: we recall one home-made training video that reduced its viewers to helpless laughter because the cameraman had decided to frame the speaker with the library's potted plants, giving the impression of an intrepid jungle explorer rather than the manager of an excellent LIS.

Open days

Open days and fairs are always a valuable promotional tool. The lure of refreshments or a few free gifts may be too much for many to resist at the end of lunchtime! Suppliers may be able to defray some of the costs; they may attend to demonstrate their offerings, or offer limited time passwords allowing users to try out and experiment with the services. Open days have the advantage of allowing LIS staff and users to meet in a more informal atmosphere than the normal transaction of LIS and client – but be prepared for someone to attend bearing a real enquiry that needs urgent attention! Other pitfalls include the technical expert who has difficult questions about the computer infrastructure, or can describe other and better ways of achieving the same result. Many suppliers are expert at dealing with this kind of visitor and are well worth having along.

(Although if you invite more than one, perhaps because of the need for several subject specialist suppliers, it is good etiquette to tell them that their competitors are coming too.)

Internal contractors and suppliers

In many organizations some of the services that the LIS relies on have been outsourced, or are provided by some kind of direct supply organization in place of a former corporate department. Many bodies, from companies to central and local government, have contracted out the supply of computing and telecommunications services. You could also find that training and other relevant services have been outsourced.

If this is the case in your organization, you clearly need to hold discussions with these bodies early in the development of your plans. You may have to set up formal negotiations for EIS components to be carried on the network, especially if more capacity will be needed to connect to the internet or external networks (such as JANET or the Government Secure Intranet), or if you will be asking for additional facilities such as streaming video or want network security settings to be changed.

The exact procedures to be followed will of course vary from organization to organization. We recommend that you should aim to have a service level agreement (SLA) at the end of negotiations for technical facilities, stating clearly what the supplier will provide and what the obligations of the LIS are in return. The SLA needs to be quite precise, to the extent of specifying items such as the supported file formats, the capacity of internet links, or the features such as ActiveX or JavaScript to be supported or prohibited by the security settings. Although there is a view that the measure is meaningless (because it relies on data transfer over the internet, which cannot be controlled from within the organization), it is worth trying to include a measure of the speed of download of web pages, at least from internal servers.

Less obvious is the need to consider other contractors who may feel that their position is being eroded by your new service. A photocopying contractor may feel that the ability to print off articles from the EIS will undermine the level of demand for copies. Your legal department or your procurement experts may have a view on the intellectual property licensing aspects of the service that may result in the need for a re-statement of the conditions of use of journal, newspaper and book extracts.

Your telecommunications supplier may find that demand has shifted as a result of your service, and that data communications have grown while the number of fax machines required has fallen. The stationery supplier may find additional demand for printer paper, although this may be met by diverting supplies from photocopiers. Users may start asking for more floppy disks and CD-ROMs.

External suppliers

We have already looked at how external suppliers can help in making presentations to your users. Now we consider how you may want to bring them into your planning in more general ways.

There are few offerings on the market that are likely to satisfy all your requirements, unless you have a very narrow range of subject interests and only one publisher whose journals and books you buy. More likely you will find that you will be dealing with a range of suppliers of different types.

The kinds of supplier of e-content

Although it may appear that there are a number of similar suppliers of electronic information services, they actually fall into a number of different categories. These are usefully distinguished in a recent article (Inger, 2001) which groups them as follows:

- content hosts, where a site provides publishers with a hosting service that publishes their output: there is usually no attempt by the site to select material or to apply any kind of quality certificate, although in one case a site has created a level of site quality that is attractive to publishers in its subject field

- publication portals, where a website provides access to a subscription agent's services and additional features such as abstracts: hyperlinks give access to full text on publishers' sites (as opposed to the model above, which itself houses the text)
- full-text content aggregators, where a site licenses content from many sources and sells it on an individual basis rather than as subscriptions to particular titles.

It is likely that you will need to use a combination of these services to obtain the electronic content that you require. In effect, your e-service will become a content aggregator tailored to the requirements of your users, drawing on other portals and suppliers to provide content.

Conditions of use and cost

This has one particular problem. Only your most sophisticated users are likely to realize that a variety of sources have been brought together. Many of your customers will have problems in understanding that different conditions apply to the various elements of the service. So customers trying to put together a research portfolio may find different conditions apply to related items from different suppliers, or that different pricing options apply. It will be a particular problem where material is being paid for using the third model, and no subscription is taken. Any use or re-use of the material is likely to be charged for, since this is the only revenue source for the content creator from the customer LIS. The reasons for apparent anomalies must be explained to users of your service, and their compliance requested.

By way of benefit, however, those services that are offering full-text access to individual articles, rather than selling subscriptions, are able to price the items according to the size of the purchasing organization and based on an assessment of the real effect of the purchase on their revenue stream. This looks likely to be of most benefit to the smallest and largest purchasers – the smallest because they would be unlikely to buy a subscription anyway for a one-off requirement, and the largest because of the power of buying consortia to negotiate subscription prices with the suppliers.

This model has also produced a remarkable amount of free content – the Highwire science and medicine portal is one notable example, providing a long page of links to such content (**http://highwire.stanford.edu/lists/freeart.dtl**) as well as to paid-for content elsewhere on the site. But a frequent feature of free content is that it is not available for a period that coincides with the publisher's view of the time that sales of the journal are likely to make an important contribution to revenue. This model is therefore useful for research and academic applications, but considerably less useful for business and other current requirements.

Keeping in touch and up to date

You are also likely to need to keep in frequent touch with your suppliers. Formal review meetings will be complemented by more informal meetings, such as trade fairs and visits. Suppliers often save their new developments for the major international exhibitions and conferences, including those of electronic publishing as well as those of the electronic information industries.

It is important to ensure that you observe the rules of propriety in this area, just as you doubtless would in any other commercial negotiations. Because this is an exciting and new area, it is possible to be carried away, ignoring the proper conventions. Some intriguing deals were offered by some now-defunct suppliers in the early days of library automation when desktop computers were not the commonplace item of furniture they now are, and they would probably not have passed muster with any procurement team.

In a book such as this it is impossible to provide up-to-date information on publishers' current offers and the conditions of use of their service. You should ensure that you look frequently at relevant discussion groups to see what is available on the market, and what other users' views of these offers are. These groups will also help to keep you abreast of current thinking around the building and management of electronic library and information services. The notes for this chapter provide more details of the major discussion lists. Many of them allow subscribers to opt to receive a mailing each time a posting is made by one of the members. It can be interesting to follow a discussion in real time when a publisher announces a new offer or policy decision, but it can be intrusive to receive all postings on busy lists.

External customers

You will also need to take account of any external customers of your LIS. Note that an 'external customer' may be neither external nor a customer in your thinking, but the conditions under which you obtain electronic content may require you to see things differently.

First, where is 'external'? The definition is likely to have as much to do with geography as it is with membership of your organization. Some suppliers are willing to license and supply information content to all members of an organization – the registered students and faculty of a university or college, employees of a firm – without being concerned where they are physically located. Others will take a view based on geographic clusters of users, arguing that different offices of the same company are separate groups and must be licensed separately. In one case known to us, there was a debate over the concept of site licensing because a college had been built on both sides of a former public street that had become a path between two buildings on the campus.

If the physical location of the user is a problem, it will need to be resolved by a combination of licence conditions and electronic control of access to the server that carries the e-content. At Yale University, for example, proxy servers are used to cope with requests from users working off campus. The IP address of the user's computer may need to be verified by some proxy server software, so that it is an advantage when patrons subscribe to those ISPs that provide fixed addresses – but these are relatively few and further authentication using passwords may be required if numbers of library patrons are not to find themselves unable to obtain remote access.

However users accessing via some internet services may find it difficult to establish any usable connection: AOL users have experienced particular problems. (At the time of writing it is unclear whether these have been resolved in Version 7.)

Consider whether you need to issue instructions or even suitably configured freeware dialler and terminal software; if your organization has people who travel regularly and are likely to try to dial in to your e-service using a laptop in a hotel, or from a cybercafé, then you need to provide clear instructions and as much help as possible. It is probably easier to sort this out before it is needed than try to provide a helpdesk service to someone calling from their mobile phone in the middle of a busy cybercafé!

Second, what is a 'customer'? Are all members of the organization entitled to use the service, or only those who are bona fide students or employees? The narrow definition might exclude use of the LIS for commercial research purposes, even when this was taking place in a university department; or it might exclude consultants from using the library in the organization that was employing their services.

Definitions and agreements require caution and advice

We constantly urge caution with contracts and with service level agreements. Take care that the text of the agreement reflects what you want and need, not what the supplier wants to give you. Suppliers are not in the business of underhand treatment of their clients, but they do not read minds, and may genuinely believe that their standard offer meets your requirements if they are not told otherwise. If you are unclear about the definitions, ask, and insist that the explanation is recorded so it can be examined in any future case of doubt. If you are in any doubt, seek a qualified legal opinion. (Just as you believe that lawyers should use expert LIS professional help to seek legal information, so they believe you should use professional legal services instead of guessing the answers!) This is a specialist field, so be prepared to suggest that your generalist lawyer should seek a specialist in electronic information and intellectual property rights if he or she is uncertain.

Once you have your definition and the technical means to serve external users, establish what level of service (if any) you wish or are able to provide. Access to library catalogues on the world wide web is now a commonplace, and there is a substantial amount of archived research material and grey literature available on the web too. But you may have to spend considerable time – and staff resources – on providing access to published material. Do not underestimate this time and these resources, or their cost.

Keeping in touch

As with the suppliers, you will need to maintain contact with your external customers. Even where they are internal customers working from off your premises, they will need to know different ways of using the service. A bulletin or a public web page (from which, obviously, you will omit any real passwords!) will help users to understand how they reach the service. It will also provide a useful and permanent source to tell users how sources can be accessed, and to remind them about the conditions of use (such as restrictions on printing and copying articles) that may apply. Yale University, for example, provides information for users telling them how to use the secure and non-secure proxy servers, and how different routines may apply in various situations (such as telephone calling from a remote location or trying to make access using another university network).

Summary

In this chapter we have seen that a number of players need to be involved in planning an EIS. In dealing with all of them, a number of common themes have emerged:

- Communication is most important, and will ensure that energy can be devoted to building and improving service rather than fire fighting to keep the service running as users encounter difficulties.

- Helping users understand the possibilities and conditions is an important result of good communication.
- The ways of achieving that communication are likely to be through several simultaneous approaches to your target audience. Think widely, and use the most cost-effective means that you can identify that will allow you and your audience to come in direct contact and discussion.
- There are likely to be technical and legal obstacles to providing a seamless service to all potential users. Make sure you know what they are, and explain them as simply as possible to patrons. If there is a way round them using a program or script that you can provide, then make sure it is readily available.

6

BUDGETING FOR YOUR E-INFORMATION SERVICE

In this chapter we look at budgeting, and the business case for building an electronic information service. We shall be looking at:

- the business case and business plan
- what should be included in your budget
- licensing
- the costing model
- dependencies within your organization
- timescales and your business plan
- charging for services
- developments and renewal – the business scenario
- measuring use of the service
- coping together – library consortia for e-service purchasing.

The business case and business plan

If you need the bottom line, then you need read no further in this chapter, because here is the lesson learnt from the electronic library projects reported in print so far: you cannot make major savings simply by switching to electronic materials. This begs the question: why do it at all then? We shall come to that later in this chapter.

It might appear that the provision of e-resources should make little difference to the budgeting process for managing library services. The same considerations that apply to the selection of a particular journal or book title would surely carry across to the purchasing process for electronic titles. However electronic services have a number of characteristics that make it more complex to establish the business case for subscription. We shall see in this chapter that there are hidden costs in many parts of the process of establishing and maintaining an electronic collection, and that you may not be able to realize some of the anticipated savings from reducing your paper stack.

Nevertheless there is a business case to be argued. If there were no other benefits to offset the costs, nobody would build an electronic collection, after all. The discussion here cannot suit every situation in every sector – and it is certainly easier to develop e-collections in sectors where funding is readily available rather than needing to be found from operating profits elsewhere in the organization. By attempting to determine added value, and to derive a benefit from it that can offset cost, it is possible to attempt a convincing case to put to financial managers.

The preparation of an outline business plan is a useful exercise for e-library proposals, since the full costs and the growing benefits will not be felt in a single financial year. Preparing a proper plan will force you to predict the length of time that you expect to keep current technology levels and platforms, and to include upgrade or replacement costs in the mix. Looking at the likely dates of availability for the components of the service will force realistic predictions of the date when benefits may begin to accrue. Making a realistic estimate of the time taken to establish a rights management system to the satisfaction of all parties will allow more accurate prediction of the dates when services will be added to the system, bringing new costs and setting the clock running towards measuring the benefits.

Treat the business plan as a serious tool: it will need to be drawn up according to whatever internal standards you use, or, failing that, imagine that you are presenting this plan to the local bank manager and use one of the many titles on starting a small business to help you plan. The office politician in you will decide whether there are any natural allies in this process, be that a senior champion, a friendly IT department or even the finance team themselves.

What should be included in your budget?

Finding out what should be purchased

Costs can be looked at as falling into two major areas: start-up and ongoing. Looked at differently, they might divide in three ways: people, materials and space. Information technology costs may be provided centrally or fall to the library; and then, to make life difficult and to make it incomprehensible to finance managers, there are costs to do with things you cannot see and cannot consume directly, such as licences.

If you are establishing a precise budget, things are then further complicated by the pricing systems adopted by publishers, both for electronic services and for the associated print service that supports many e-services.

With this kind of complexity, a sound first principle is not to plan to spend money on what is not needed. In other words, what is the requirement? We have advocated the use of information audits in various publications (Pantry and Griffiths, 1998; Pantry and Griffiths, 2002) as a means of establishing user needs, allowing the LIS to identify the most cost-effective services that will meet those requirements. An audit is likely to identify both a need expressed as a requirement for current information on particular topics at regular intervals (daily business news, digest of the scientific weeklies each Friday morning) or for a particular title on publication. The list is likely to be long in many organizations, but this exercise will show up:

- requirements for particular titles
- requirements for particular subject information, and frequency of those requirements.

At the current stage of development we believe that for LIS use the vast majority of materials identified in this process will be periodical titles. The market for e-books is still too immature, and because they are frequently tied to particular hardware platforms the LIS may find it needs to spend yet more money on handheld computers or other new equipment. The fact that so many of these items of equipment will be highly desirable to users may make the potential for theft so high that the LIS is unwilling to bear or insure that risk.

Checking the costs

Checking the electronic availability of individual periodical titles may be a long process. Printed directories are unlikely to capture the speed of change. A combination of advice from your journal suppliers and checks of publishers' websites will go a long way towards establishing which titles you can expect to obtain in electronic form, and the costs of taking these services.

Possible surprise: these checks will also reveal the answer to another question, which is the publisher's policy on making electronic and paper versions available at the same time. For reasons to do with safeguarding the revenue stream, or from other motives, a number of publishers impose a moratorium during which only the paper version circulates. Typically, a large academic publisher may set a one-year period at the end of which the electronic version appears – Elsevier is one such. This policy may suit fine for an academic library, since it will provide access to an archived copy at exactly the time when circulation of the journal parts is likely to be diminishing, and consideration given to permanent binding. But for a company where information is valuable only when it is new, that policy is unworkable. Commercial research-based information work is forced to continue using paper when electronic access would be far better suited to the needs of the user and the LIS.

Next surprise: many publishers do not make a reduction for taking electronic copies only of their titles. Although they may give you electronic access for nothing, some of them charge extra for the privilege. A few of them tempt you to sign up to their entire catalogue of publications at what appears to be a bargain price (but there is always a catch, as we see below). Just sometimes you will discover that journals are available free of charge. Most of these are official publications: the days of free content seem to be slowly diminishing as the free web publication model begins to become unworkable.

A list of key titles together with the costs of supply will show you the marginal costs of adding electronic service to the LIS. This will demonstrate the costs – if any – of providing electronic access to your LIS's list of key periodicals. Store this information to be fed into the business case model.

Tangible resources

At the end of this part of the process you will have an idea of the cost of providing the key materials your users require in electronic form. You will also have some idea whether it is possible to discard any current printed material (either in its totality or in part, by reducing the number of paid subscriptions bought or by shortening the run held). On the assumption that you can also produce a cost figure for your use of building space and services, this information will give a cost for space saved. However do not draw the line yet; the space you save may be needed for equipment.

In order to run an e-service, the LIS must have equipment that is able to provide fast and full access. This is likely to mean paying for some or all of the following:

- a server
- terminals
- printers
- cabling and access points
- high-speed internet access
- terminal adapters, cable modems, or other communications equipment.

In addition to these hardware costs, you may need to account for:

- software – even open source software needs installation, and the new services may need a higher version of Internet Explorer than your intranet does

- space to put hardware, and to store software and documentation – even if not prime office space
- connection to office networks, and perhaps the cost of additional modules for the library management system to provide an online catalogue
- technical skills to make the equipment connect to itself, to users, and to the internet, and technical skills to configure the system
- additional services such as air-conditioning improvements – although equipment is less sensitive, and puts out less heat than it did, older buildings cannot cope
- additional telecommunications services
- security, physical or electronic.

Most of these are items that you can touch, and probably sell on or write off over a period of time (although used air conditioning may be an exception). You should check how much adequate telecommunications will cost, especially if you decide that you need two-channel ISDN running constantly to give you fast access.

Alternative approaches

You may decide that this is all too much, and that it would be easier to pay someone else to do it. Clearly, outsourcing is an option, particularly in the smaller LIS where staff time is at a premium as well as the required skills. In this case many of the costs will be transparent and if the specification is well written it should be possible to arrive at an agreed price quickly. However costs such as telecommunications will still appear in this model, as may software and other licence costs. In addition, the LIS will still need to account for the costs of the information, as we shall see shortly.

In 2001 a further option emerged with the appearance of Application Service Providers in the LIS market. While the downturn in the computer market has been quite harsh to this sector, it may be that in specialist areas such as LIS it is fully viable. Put simply, rather than maintaining IT equipment on your premises and managing the software and hardware, you contract with a supplier who maintains all the equipment. Your data is managed by the contractor who is responsible for backing up data and clearing corrupt files. Your LIS then manages the data itself, adding, amending and deleting it as required.

So much for the cost of setting the service up. What about running costs?

Operational expenses

Many of the costs of operating the service are well known and appear in all libraries. Where documents emerge from the electronic system on to paper costs are incurred as with published documents: postage, fax, paper, ink and so on, and envelopes, files or other containers.

Training and publicity costs are significant and must be accounted for. A helpdesk may be needed to guide users. When we look at convergence in libraries – the joining of library services with other departments, typically computer services in much of UK higher education, into a single unit – we find that many basic enquiries are answered by a new breed of worker who combines LIS professional skills with IT or other knowledge, and who is able to deal with many user enquiries. However just as major IT incidents are handled by a central enterprise helpdesk, so there will be more complex training and user enquiries that need more advanced LIS skills to be resolved. Thus an element of quite senior management time needs to be built into the model along with the more obvious costs of service.

Do not forget the cost of out-of-hours support. Council IT departments may work five days a week for seven and a half hours a day, but public libraries are open far longer than that. Many university libraries are open until very late at night, but major system failures at peak examination times will not go unremarked.

The following table (Table 6.1) illustrates some of the potential costs incurred. Note that once the initial costs have been met, there are new and ongoing costs if access is to be maintained. Depending on your organization or community's arrangements, there may be further ongoing costs such as equipment maintenance (typically 15% of capital costs in the second and following years).

Table 6.1 *Typical start-up and ongoing operational costs for an e-information service*

	Start-up costs	Ongoing costs
People	Project manager	Helpdesk staff
	Specialist IT	
Equipment	Server	Communications
	Software	
	Terminals	
	Printers	
	Cabling	
Space	Storage	

But now what of the invisible costs?

Licensing

The use of e-journals and other electronic services is regulated by licence. The terms may not be negotiable. As we saw above, in a number of cases the electronic version is supplied only on condition that a subscription to the paper version is maintained. There may even be an additional charge for networking the electronic version. The agreement must be examined for each publisher to discover which arrangement is used and what other conditions are imposed.

There are further differences between products as some offer licences based on the size of the entire network that will carry the product, while others offer licences based on the number of simultaneous users. The numbers of users that represent price thresholds also tends to vary from producer to producer. Thus a network of 100 users may simply represent 'more than ten users' for one product but for another it would be critical to know whether 100 or 101 users were present because a threshold in price would be crossed.

It may be possible to configure workstations on the network to prevent access by more than a certain number of users to a given title and thus keep costs down. If the information product and the network cannot be configured in this way it may mean restricting the service to standalone access.

There are likely to be variations in the conditions regarding the use of the service by customers who are not within the same site as the LIS, and possibly regarding use by those who are visitors rather than members of the parent body. The definition of 'site' may vary. Some suppliers will regard faculty members working at home as being on the same site as the LIS, others will not. Some suppliers will regard adjacent office buildings as a single site if they share a computer network. Beware: in one case we found, apparently adjacent buildings were divided by what had been a public street so that the telecommunications between them had to be managed via telephone rather than laying a direct network cable, and they became two separate sites.

The questions concerning licensing when establishing cost benefits are:

- Does the paper product have to be maintained?
- Is there a premium for electronic use?
- Is it possible to license a number of simultaneous users, or must every post on the network be licensed?
- What are the price thresholds for savings (or additional costs)?
- Is it possible to configure the network in order to avoid going through a threshold?

Access to back issues

The purchase of a periodical enables a library to provide continuous access for as long as it cares to retain the parts or bound volumes. Clearly, for a title purchased only in electronic format this is not true since there is no physical volume to consult. The library will instead need to use the electronic service to provide access to the back issues of periodicals.

Publishers have varying approaches to this requirement, particularly in terms of cancellations and where titles transfer between publishers.

Example: the publisher provides access to a back file provided that the customer maintains a current subscription. This may allow the library to use electronic archives of an earlier date than any subscription registered. In this case, what happens if the library cancels? Does it lose access to the back runs, and in particular to the journal during the dates for which it subscribed? If so, the library is in effect tied in to future subscription for as long as the title remains important, and this sum must be provided for in future budgets. A number of publishers have recognized that this is a potential area of conflict and their contracts now make clear that a cancelling subscriber maintains the right of access to archives of the years that it has already purchased.

Example: the journal changes from one publisher to another with different arrangements for access to back files. What are the library's rights in this situation? What does the contract allow for?

Example: the journal ceases publication. What are the rights of existing subscribers to retain access to back files? Is there a cost? Can the subscribers obtain an electronic archive to maintain on their system?

As subscribers have begun to realize with the failure of netLibrary, these are not trivial questions (Fialkoff, 2001). In that case, the loss was e-books, rather than e-journals, but the University of Texas was reported to have lost access to 35,000 items. The contract terms are critically important, and issues such as escrow must be taken into account. (In other words, does the contract make provision for continuing access to the e-content through a third party in the case that the vendor fails?) We indicate a number of such areas that need to be considered in our works on service level agreements (Pantry and Griffiths, 2001) and on the management of internet services (Griffiths, 2000), but no advice in printed form can take the place of the opinions of your legal adviser. Those opinions are, after all, what he or she is prepared to defend or prosecute. Only when you have taken your lawyer's advice will you know how much support you can expect in maintaining your service. What you may have to urge is that if he or she is not an expert in the areas of intellectual property and electronic service provision then further opinion must be sought from expert counsel.

The costing model

As you were warned at the outset of this chapter, a major problem with making the business case for the e-library is that it does not appear to save money, at least at present. It may thus be difficult to argue for developing an e-service on purely economic grounds. Unless you can obtain a deal from a particular supplier, there will probably have to be other circumstances to reinforce the argument for the electronic service: for example, you may have particular constraints on space, or there may be geographic or security reasons that prevent users from having the fullest access to services. These cases may change the argument sufficiently to make the service an economic proposition. Otherwise you may have to argue on grounds such as modernization of services, widening the range of available resources or investment with a view to longer-term savings, because in the short term the e-service is likely to cost more.

The final report of the e-Lib project puts it succinctly: '. . . electronic media do not save money or library space and are not likely to in the near future' (ESYS Consulting, 2001). In the case of the higher education establishments looked at by e-Lib, the reasons for this include the following:

- Electronic sources continue to overlap with conventional printed materials so the take-up is inevitably limited.
- There is a need to provide additional computing facilities to provide access to the journals.
- The back runs available in electronic form are limited, typically three to five years, so that conventional materials will be required for a long time in the future.

If we look at a wider area than that typically covered by higher education establishments in the UK, there are some further reasons why take-up may be slow.

Publishers typically address the academic market rather than the business market. In business, the need is for recent information rather than an archive of material that typically remains useful for five to ten years.

Business information has an immediacy that is not found in other fields, and it does not generally go through the sort of review that is found in STM literature, for example.

But you will look hard for the electronic service that meets this need. In order to meet their need for a viable title, publishers will typically place an embargo on electronic archives of their journals for a period of a year or more (Spiteri, 2001). That goes against what business librarians need. So in a business environment you are likely to find that you can provide news services and current affairs feeds at a reasonable price, but that you cannot license many of the sources that you want to provide because of the time delay before they become available.

Some publishers, of which the *Economist* is one example, make their content available on a paying basis. However there is a benefit to maintaining paper subscriptions as well.

The *Economist* currently offers paper edition subscribers free access to premium content on its website after registration, paying subscriptions to electronic content on a weekly, monthly or annual basis (monthly being twice the weekly cost, and annual 12 times that cost), and, via Northern Light, purchase of individual articles at a one-off fee ($2.95 as at January 2002, but this may change now that Northern Light has refocused on paid-for services).

The pay-off may actually be in the form of improved service at an increased price. The information manager of one multinational research organization noted (Duncan, 1997): 'We can now provide access to a much wider range of information on many different media, but whether this actually gets people what they need more effectively is not easy to measure.'

One problem is that users believe they can find the information they need free of charge on the internet, so that information does not appear to be worth paying for through licensing or other arrangements. It is forgotten that 'you only get what you pay for' and information service managers need to explain why there is still a need for paying access to electronic services.

Dependencies in the organization

Your budget and business plan must, of course, fit into the requirements of your organization. This means, for example, presenting the figures in the required format (such as accruals accounting, where income and expenditure are shown at the point they are incurred rather than at the time the invoices are cleared) or within the required timescales, such as the organization's financial year.

This may not be quite so simple. Accounting for a subscription causes problems within an accruals system because it is delivered at intervals but paid for in advance, while consumption of information that is not part of a subscription (such as use of online information retrieval services) is unpredictable. So how can you predict the figures?

The answer may be that you cannot, other than basing them on the pattern that has been set by the existing service. Paper subscriptions and electronic subscriptions may turn out to be part of the same thing, as many publishers combine the two. The problem for accruals is that while you may argue for an annual subscription to a monthly publication to be accounted for as 12 monthly instalments paid on a given date, the electronic version is consumed at an irregular rate, and the quantity available increases gradually through the year as new issues are added. Just to add a touch of complexity, the electronic issues may not become available at the same time as the printed equivalent. It may be easiest to ignore these difficulties, since resolving them seems not to add much to the sum of knowledge about the benefits derived from the library. It would be as well to square this with the finance section, but they may well grasp at the simple solution if you begin to explain the complexities.

The use of financial years based around fiscal years is a further problem in those organizations where this does not coincide with the calendar year, or rather the subscription year. The academic year in many countries has long been out of kilter with the calendar and systems are in place to deal with this. But it remains worth ensuring that there are no problems from the financial department's viewpoint where the relative uncertainty of e-content subscriptions is introduced.

Timescales and your business plan

A different but related problem relates to the timescale of the business plan. For a number of reasons your plan will need to cover more than one financial year. Among the reasons are that you will clearly not be able to make savings by a total switch on a given day from printed to electronic resources; that you will need to phase the introduction of new services; and that you may well be unable to access electronic versions of paper journals for a period of time after publication that is set by the publisher.

Charging for services

Many organizations now expect their LIS to act in a commercial fashion, at least to the extent of recharging for services even if not providing a directly commercial service against hard payment. You will need to ensure that the terms of your contracts do not prevent you from doing this using electronic services.

The situation will vary from contract to contract, and may vary from country to country in respect of the types of LIS or research that are included or excluded from the scope of any restrictions that apply for legal or contractual reasons.

One of the most likely pitfalls is where the service that you are offering could be construed as re-publishing the information that you have licensed, or as infringing copyright on information that is restricted by contract or law. (For example, the effects of the new Australian Digital Agenda Act should be examined in the context of its definition of commercial research, and the exclusion of that research from fair dealing concessions.) If you have any doubts, our advice is once again to seek expert counsel from your legal adviser.

Developments and renewal – the business scenario

The business plan that you propose and adopt for an e-service needs to be flexible. The pace of change in the industry that will supply your service is fast and sometimes brutal:

- The number of content aggregators and journal vendors has reduced through mergers and consolidation, and the trend may be set to continue.
- New deals become available and others are lost (sometimes suddenly, as with netLibrary), but often with additional costs or contractual conditions.
- Changes in costs – generally upwards – affect the economics of information service provision.

In addition to dealing with these developments, the business model that you propose must reflect the change from payment for ownership to payment for continuing access to information.

As a result, there will be some major changes in the way that your plans are drawn up in comparison with the way financial plans for a paper-based library are constructed.

The budget will be less predictable in the sense that some leeway must be retained to cope with changes in pricing strategies. Buying decisions may become irreversible: some suppliers, for example, will not allow an LIS that buys a total access package to its titles to then revert to purchase of individual titles. (As a result, the choice is between continuing to pay for the package at whatever price it commands, or losing access to important titles.) An element of the LIS budget becomes dedicated to maintaining access to basic materials.

From the accounting department's point of view this may not be good news, since in order to maintain existing levels of information provision, a guaranteed sum is required in each succeeding financial year. The LIS must incorporate this baseline figure into its budget predictions before any new material is allowed for.

This is not necessarily good news for the LIS: 'libraries can tie up the whole budget and can't add anything new at all', according to one commentator (Landesman, 2001). Where budgets are reduced, hard choices have to be made.

Case study: GALILEO

GALILEO, the state-wide database network of Georgia (USA), became subject to budget cuts in planning for Financial Years 2002 and 2003, experiencing successive and cumulative cuts of 2.5%. In November 2001, the library director of Augusta State University warned that the system would have to drop one database from its lineup because of rising costs. The scheme's communities had generally received flat funding over the previous years, but the two database suppliers (ProQuest and EBSCOhost) had continued to provide additional content, which required more money. Groups within GALILEO compared databases from the two vendors, assessing the scope, content, usability and other evaluation criteria to help the GALILEO Steering Committee decide between ProQuest and EBSCOhost databases.

According to the Virtual Library Development Specialist for GALILEO, budget reductions, coming as a result of the economic downturn, declining revenues, and a decline in the value of endowments at private colleges and universities, had underscored the need to choose between these two popular suites of databases or a combination of the database offerings. ProQuest and EBSCOhost databases were targeted because such a large portion of the scheme's funding was going towards buying these databases and because of the degree of overlap of journal titles. The GALILEO administrators stressed that this was not a choice they relished making, but it was necessary to demonstrate good stewardship of the allocated resources.

The GALILEO newsletter reported (*GALILEO Planet*, 2002) that various members and groups within GALILEO's communities had contributed their own evaluations and opinions to help in selecting between the databases.

The criteria that the GALILEO Collection Development Committee reviewed in reaching their decision on future purchases were:

- user comments
- database overlap

- search results data
- database usage statistics
- information about embargoes and exclusive titles.

In addition the two vendors were asked to make presentations to the Committee. Eventually the Committee recommended that if at all possible, GALILEO should keep all databases except for Newspaper Abstracts and Dissertation Abstracts. The Committee recommended other less desirable alternatives, should funding not be available, and directed its chairman to negotiate further with both vendors. Following these discussions, the Georgia Public Library Service announced it would provide additional funding from LSTA funds to support the continuation of both products. The proposals were finally agreed in December 2001.

Measuring use of the service

One of the problems with a service that is provided electronically without the need for the patron to visit the LIS for every transaction is the difficulty of establishing viable measurements of use. The system may well be able to provide raw data on the number of consultations of the databases taking place, and may support the collection of information about individual users' activities, or at least the activity of particular terminals.

This lack of information of course makes it more difficult to demonstrate usage in order to establish savings or increased value. A recent study at Texas A&M University found that the statistics on the use of electronic journals were inconclusive. It would need suppliers to provide more information before any conclusions could be drawn about savings through transferring to electronic-only subscriptions. The University had decided that this change would be possible in some subject areas but not in others, for example in economics but not in political science (Gyeszly, 2001). This poses a further decision: is it better to collect this data where it is available and to take action on it for the subject areas concerned, or should all subject areas be treated the same? There is clear scope for complaints of unfair treatment for particular subjects, but this seems to be inevitable until better information is available.

It is also difficult to establish whether the length of time of use is related in any way to the value added. Long and expensive searches of external databases may reflect the delivery of extensive and valuable literature searches, or they may simply demonstrate a need for user training in search techniques and the formats available for cost-effective downloading of the records retrieved. Long connection times to internal databases may reflect changes in user habits: if there is no charge for service, users may simply remain logged in for long periods without active use. This may make no difference to these careless users, but may distort the statistics of use.

Other potential users may be locked out by selfish users because of limits on the number of simultaneous users of a database or a CD-ROM, perhaps leading to demands that a more expensive licence be purchased. If other users are unable to make searches, these, obviously, will not feature in statistics of use. Users may consult other databases outside the e-service, or go to informal information sources such as their colleagues, reducing the value obtained from the service.

E-suppliers are now able to provide statistics of use for many resources, but the complaint remains that they are inconsistent and do not allow proper comparison of the use of services (Pinfield, 2001). The EQUINOX project, funded by the Telematics for Libraries programme funded by the European Commission, has developed a set of proposed performance indicators for electronic libraries (**http://equinox.dcu.ie/reports/pilist. html**). Earlier useful studies in this area include MIEL (Management Information in Electronic Libraries) (Brophy and Wynne, 1997) and the work based at Albany University on the Developing National Library Network Statistics & Performance Measures project (**www.albany.edu/~imlsstat/**). See, for example, Bertot, McClure and Ryan, 1999.

See also 'Evaluating, monitoring and measuring your e-services' in Chapter 7.

Coping together – library consortia for e-service purchasing

Libraries have been acting together in order to obtain improved terms or to make the operation of a joint activity more efficient for the best part of 70 years: in that sense consortia are nothing new.

However they have become an important feature of purchasing digital services for libraries in a number of countries. In the UK they have become a major force since the mid-1990s, and have also introduced variety to the consortium model in terms of their management and governance. But we are less concerned here about the issues concerning the accountability of the management committee or other parts of the organization. (See Ball and Pye, 2000, for a discussion.)

These consortia are a feature in many countries, and in many cases are actively encouraged by publishers and suppliers. For example, the Japanese company Maruzen, which has developed from one of the first companies to introduce European knowledge and information to Japan following the reopening of the country in the 1860s, now includes a substantial bookshop and library supply business which offers to help build purchasing consortia to use its Marunet e-services supply arm (**www.maruzen.co.jp/home-eng/ marunet.html#3**).

Consortia offer a number of strategic and operational advantages to LIS that introduce e-services. They improve value for money not only by combining the purchasing power of the individual libraries but also by reducing the duplication of effort that the members expend on the purchasing process. They have a greater profile than their individual members in lobbying for progress in developing suitable commercial and legal frameworks for the development of services. And, as one commentator puts it, they pool their individual uncertainties in order to move forward more positively (Woodward, 2001).

Besides the advantages of cost gained from consortium negotiations, further benefits can be derived from consortium working, depending on the permissions and agreements that are given. Where one institution suffers a technical breakdown, for example, where the licences allow this, users can be served from a different location until the service can be restored. Interlibrary loan procedures may also be simplified by the existence of the consortium, especially where procedures and conventions may not yet be fully worked out as with interlending of electronic items.

Consortia are also playing an important role in setting standards for usage measurement and other related activities in the field of e-services that we considered above. ICOLC, the International Coalition of Library Consortia, has developed guidelines for service measurement (ICOLC, 2001), which by January 2002 had been adopted by 75 consortia on four continents. The Graduate School of Library and Information Science at the University of Illinois at Urbana-Champaign provides a collection of useful documents for the establishment and management of such groups (Sloan, n.d).

Summary

This chapter has looked at a number of concerns in the field of business planning and costing of e-services. It has indicated a number of issues that you should be considering, if only to ensure that they are not potential show-stoppers in your situation, and pointed out the sources of further information about those that will require further investigation.

We have seen that:

- There is unlikely to be a quick financial gain from the introduction of electronic services, but
- Other benefits make it an attractive proposition for many libraries to develop them.
- Easy sources of financial returns, such as the sale of information, may be prohibited by the terms of the agreement for your e-service, so
- Other managers in your organization may need to be educated about the realities of developing electronic services.
- Measurement of the service may also be difficult, especially if it is to support financial investment in the service or to illustrate a return, but

- Membership of a consortium brings the strong likelihood of being able to sign up to common standards and to gain benefits and efficiencies as a result.

7

KEEPING IN TOUCH WITH YOUR CUSTOMERS

In this chapter we look at the important tasks that you should be starting as your e-information service rolls out to your LIS users. They are things that you should already have been doing with your traditional services, but because this is such a fast-moving arena, it is doubly important that you plan these activities carefully.

We look at:

- evaluating, monitoring and measuring the services you offer
- keeping yourself and your customers aware of developments in external suppliers' services
- checking how these services could meet your customers' needs
- introducing new services into your e-portfolio.

Evaluating, monitoring and measuring your e-services

The need for evaluation

Once the services are established you will constantly need to assess, evaluate and monitor them. Services cannot be regarded as set in concrete. Many new and competing services and products are constantly arriving on the scene and you will need to consider them for their potential impact on the service that you are currently offering. Each part of the service should be examined in detail, and evaluated asking questions such as these:

- Is this product still needed?
- If so, is it needed in the same format?
- Should it be produced by the same staff member or team?
- Could it be carried out somewhere else in the organization, but outside the e-information centre?
- Should it be carried out outside the organization?
- Is there a better way of getting or delivering this product or the information it provides?
- Is it being offered in the most appropriate way?
- And at the most appropriate price?

You will need to ask the same questions about any external services that may have potential for being brought into the e-information service, especially where they appear to be replacements for existing services.

Measuring use of the EIS

One means of assessing the need for a product is, of course, to look at the statistics of use. For books this can be done simply enough from loan records and date labels, and for journals there are measures like circulation lists and demand for copy articles. But how on earth can you measure use of an LIS where many of the users are not even on the same campus as the library, and don't need to visit it to use it?

This is not just a problem for digitized library collections. Managers of library websites have similar difficulties in measuring use of their sites in a meaningful way. Some sites appear to have far higher numbers of users than others, but this may be to do with the measure used – page impressions are now reckoned as a more accurate measure than, for example, a count of the number of files requested. The final measurement can be affected by, for example, the complexity of the page and whether or not a user has graphics turned on.

The considerations that apply to websites also apply to the search pages that guide users to digital materials on an LIS's website. Page impressions are more use as a measure than file requests; but because specific files are exactly what users are ultimately seeking in a digital collection, that measure becomes far more useful for measuring use of the digital materials themselves than for a standard website. (Bear in mind too that precise identification of files accessed may be needed for rights management, so it is helpful to be able to obtain a tally of the files downloaded and their identities.)

Recent versions of Webtrends and other software packages developed for website management have the ability to track users through sites, noting in particular the pages at which they entered and left. This feature is particularly helpful in identifying deep links to your collection – that is, for example, where a member of the organization has built a web page linking directly to a digitized item on your server. It will also help to locate particular pages that cause a high number of users to abandon their search, suggesting there may be a problem with the links on the page, or that there is unmet demand for materials that might be expected to appear on that page.

Looking for suitable measures

Various projects have looked at the question of measuring the use of e-services. Table 7.1 (overleaf) shows the measures proposed by the EQUINOX project, a European project, and those of the ICOLC, the International Coalition of Library Consortia, based in North American universities. Where there appears to be an equivalent measure they are shown on the same row. As will be quickly seen, most of the measures do not match, and even where there is a correlation the match is not exact. The ICOLC measures have a much greater emphasis on counting of various activities: the EQUINOX measures are ratios, even where the item being measured is the same (see, for example, the measure of the number of sessions in the third row). ICOLC does propose subdivisions of each of its measures, but they are functional divisions: by each specific database of the provider; by each institution's set of IP addresses; by total consortium; by special data element passed by subscriber (e.g., account or ID number); and by time period.

Table 7.1 *Quality management approaches to measurement*

EQUINOX	ICOLC
Number of remote sessions on electronic library services per member of the population to be served	Number of queries (searches)
	Number of menu selections
Number of sessions on each electronic library service per member of the target population.	Number of sessions (logins)
Rejected sessions as a percentage of total attempted sessions	Number of turn-aways, if relevant, as a contract limit (e.g. requests exceed simultaneous user limit)
Number of documents and entries (records) viewed per session for each electronic library service	Number of items examined (i.e. marked or selected, downloaded, viewed, e-mailed, printed)
	Citations displayed
	Full text displayed broken down by title, ISSN with title listed, or other title identifier as appropriate
	Tables of contents displayed
	Abstracts displayed
	Articles or essays, poems, chapters, etc., as appropriate, viewed (e.g. ASCII or HTML) or downloaded (e.g. PDF, e-mail)
	Other (e.g. image/AV files, ads, reviews, etc., as appropriate)
Percentage of the population reached by electronic library services	
Library computer workstation use rate	

Table 7.1 *Continued*

EQUINOX	ICOLC
Cost per session for each electronic library service	
Cost per document or entry (record) viewed for each electronic library service	
Percentage of information requests submitted electronically	
Number of library computer workstation hours available per member of the population to be served	
Percentage of total acquisitions expenditure spent on acquisition of electronic library services	
Number of attendances at formal electronic library service training lessons per member of the population to be served	
Library staff developing, managing and providing ELS and user training as a percentage of total library staff	
User satisfaction with electronic library services	

Quality management and performance management go hand in hand. They offer an additional or alternative way of assessing your services. You should become aware of the principles of quality management systems, such as *ISO 9004-2 Quality management for services* and *ISO 9001 Total quality management,* and consider their potential for your own LIS.

Building a quality management system will allow an information service to review where it is going effectively and continuously. The LIS will need to be brutal in its appraisal of the services and systems that it offers – striving to improve, through training of staff, through innovation, and through constantly asking (and answering, and acting on) the questions we pose above.

In order to achieve the quality of services and the performance measures, the customers should be aware that they too have a role to play. Customers should:

- be aware of what their information services can do – to achieve this, the LIS must commit to providing the customer with accurate and up-to-date information about services (see below 'Keeping yourself and your customers aware of developments in external suppliers' services')
- identify their information problems and needs – to achieve this, the LIS will need to help this process through information audits (see Chapter 2) and its publicity materials
- communicate these requirements to the information services staff and discuss them – in many organizations this can be done using the electronic network, such as a company intranet, and it seems very appropriate to do this for an EIS
- give feedback to the information services – again, using electronic channels where possible
- keep information staff aware of their changing subject interests – although it may be possible to track changes proactively using website statistics analysis
- involve the service in projects that have information implications – to achieve this, the LIS may need to improve its networking in the organization.

You will see from this that the customer has considerable influence on the quality of the service delivered by the LIS and EIS. Among the ways in which they achieve this are:

- making demands for improvements
- asking for services
- showing a willingness to co-operate.

User feedback as a measurement of your service

Constant dialogue with the users is essential if you are to set and maintain standards in the information services. The introduction of service level management can provide you with constant user feedback. You may wish to set up 'focus groups' which will consist of people in an organization or a community who are not only information seekers but are also the 'movers and shakers' among your users. The visible participation of these champions in the evaluation process will increase the standing and credibility of the service.

These people's participation in the political process in your user community will allow them to indicate when and where shifts in demands for information are taking place, allowing you to feed these changing needs through to the information services. You may also wish to use this 'focus group' to describe or try out new services or systems.

See also 'Measuring use of the service' in Chapter 6.

Keeping yourself and your customers aware of developments in external suppliers' services

The EIS should ideally have established criteria for the services it needs and that its users require. These provide the framework to evaluate the potential value of new external services that arrive on the scene, and to help decide whether they provide additional value at reasonable cost.

Your evaluation will pose questions such as:

- What does the new external service offer that is not already available in the services that you or your community purchase now?

- What are the plus and minus points of this service?
- Will the customers find the format difficult to use?
- If so, will the introduction of the service require additional training?
- Who will fund the training?
- Can the existing e-information service staff handle this new service, and will they need training?
- Could it be carried out outside of the e-information centre without any staff involvement – is the new service transparent and easy to use?
- Is it being offered at the most appropriate price?

You will learn about many of the new services that come to market through the professional press, through mail shots, and through trade exhibitions. If possible, aim to be at the major shows, or at least read reviews of the products there. Many suppliers keep new products or services to launch at trade shows, so it may pay to delay a purchasing decision until you are clear what products are coming to market. Suppliers' representatives will be anxious to make sure that you do not take your business elsewhere so they are likely, within reason, to indicate what new services will shortly be available if you ask.

Personal recommendations and contacts may be another source, depending on the field in which you work. In many areas of LIS work, there will be no problem in seeking to find out what services are used by successful services in your field, although of course you will respect commercial and security sensitivities in those areas where these are important.

Checking how these services could meet your customers' needs

How do the customers of your LIS want to receive information? The wired organization presents many opportunities that many of its members will not be aware of.

Remember that advances in technology – not to mention a number of landmark decisions in the licensing of intellectual rights – mean that an 'organization' in our context can mean not just a company, or a school, or a department in a local or national government body. In recent months we have seen electronic information services become available to the citizens of whole geographical areas; in the most remarkable case, the whole of Iceland has been given access to a range of publications online.

Case study – taken from a press release by Swets Blackwell

November 7, 2001

Landmark agreement for Iceland: entire population gains access to over 2000 e-journals

A groundbreaking national licence has been arranged between the National Steering Committee of Iceland and six major STM publishers. Under the terms of the agreement, Icelandic libraries, government and academic institutions, as well as private citizens, will have full text access to journals published by the following distinguished publishers: Academic Press – now part of Elsevier Science, Blackwell Publishing, S. Karger Publishers, Kluwer Academic Publishers and Springer-Verlag.

Iceland's 283,000 inhabitants can now access more than 2,000 e-journals from their offices as well as their private homes.

For the first time, publishers can analyze the "e-journal behaviour" of an entire nation.

Other interesting initiatives can be found in small countries (such as Singapore) or in defined areas of larger countries, where typically passwords are used to limit access to taxpayers or others with a proven association with the sponsoring administration.

Introducing new services

The 24/7 EIS

The nature of society has changed greatly in recent years, with many services available round the clock, seven days a week. What is the reaction of LIS faced with this requirement? Leaving aside financial factors for a moment – but acknowledging that in many communities, they are the reason that libraries are not available during the time that many people have free to consult the collections – many LIS cannot afford to ignore this need of many of their patrons. Part-time students, often coping with family and career demands, are penalized if services are not available to them. Media research is pressurized by the 24-hour products that television, radio and internet journalism provide. In many administrations, long service hours are becoming the norm and, as we note elsewhere, many local authority workers have long been used to being at work when their IT support team is taking the weekend break. New ways have to be sought to deal with this.

We discuss convergence – managing the overlaps between library services and technical support services – in Chapter 1. A group of multi-skilled staff cover the range of requirements to support patrons in their use of the basic services, but we noted in our description that the level of service offered out of core time is often quite rudimentary.

Co-operative arrangements between organizations appear to have greater potential in dealing with the problem. This can be bilateral, as with one library in London (UK) which is open 24 hours, and provides an e-mail address for technical support which is that of the technical support team in a New Zealand university, for which the library in London provides out-of-hours support. Multilateral arrangements have even greater potential (Smith, 1999). However, where the help desk customer and adviser are unknown to each other and work remotely, authentication is a problem, and where bilateral or multilateral agreements are drawn up, the parties must find ways to ensure that equal priority is given to remote users and to local callers.

Collaborative software (such as Microsoft's NetMeeting) has potential to be useful here, as does more advanced call centre software designed for helpdesk operations on websites (for example, Lucent Technologies' call centre tools). With these tools it is possible for a remote operative to see the user's terminal screen, and offer suggestions for improved search techniques or alternative databases.

Many electronic services will of course work with little or no attention at all times. Provided that technical staff can be reached quickly to restore service in the case of an interruption, there may be little need to intervene out of hours. Apart from scheduled maintenance, which many organizations carry out on an early morning during or at the end of the weekend, databases and servers can be left running continuously. Users may well accept that service on Sunday evenings will be less good than at noon on Wednesdays, but it may well be a source of delight for them that any kind of service is available at that time, particularly if it is supported by a professional helpdesk.

Communications

There is little point in introducing new services if nobody knows about them. That statement can be, and should be, read in two senses. First, you have to tell people what is available; and second, you have to make sure that they understand how the available services are relevant to them. The plans for your EIS should include a communication strategy.

Some of that strategy will be publicity in the old-fashioned and proven library sense; other parts of it will seek to ensure that users are fully informed about the services available. Use product handbooks and other training materials as well as publicity flyers to achieve this. Demonstration sessions will help users to understand what the services contain, and identify the potential contribution of those services to meeting your users' information requirements.

Suppliers are frequently willing to help with publicity events in an organization or community. Your success will bring them additional business so it can be time well spent for them. At the very least they will provide promotional literature (and perhaps some take-away items as reminders).

Some of your promotional effort may have to go into apparently simple messages, such as how to use the services. It is not instinctive to many people to use a web browser, or to know when a web address is likely to end in .com or .co.uk. People need help with what may be quite major tasks for them, such as downloading or installing viewer software (particularly Adobe Acrobat, which is widely used but a major download, and is likely to deter inexperienced users).

More of your effort needs to go into explaining any breaks in service that have to take place for improvement or re-installation of your service. At Gravelines in northern France, the library service was deliberately closed for two weeks to allow a new e-service to be completed. The time was used to provide information that whetted the public's appetite and the service re-opened to considerable demand for the range of services (Deconinck and Gauchet, 1998).

Summary

In many ways, keeping in touch with your customers is up to you – in this book we can only offer pointers to what works, and suggest the kinds of issues that should concern you, no matter what kind of LIS you work in.

We have seen that measurement is still an imprecise science, and that there is not as much information as you might wish for in order to convince your managers of the value of e-services. We have suggested that the worlds of quality management and user surveys may provide you with some useful techniques to provide such evidence. We have suggested techniques for evaluating services against user needs.

Above all, we recommend that you take every opportunity to keep yourself as well informed as possible about the available services. You act as the users' professional adviser, even if they do the searching themselves, and it is your recommendation or purchasing decision that provides the service they use. Keep aware in as many ways as possible, in order to know which offers are best for your EIS, and which existing services could be improved or replaced.

8

KEEPING ONE STEP AHEAD OF YOUR COMPETITORS

In this chapter we look at some ways of keeping ahead of the competition, and anticipating your customers' needs too. We consider:

- your networks
  - — what can they tell you?
  - — people
  - — management
  - — technical
- a way to manage the relationship with competitors and customers
- winning others across
- customers
- suppliers
- electronic journals
- using integrated services to head off customer requests
- dealing with particular users in organizations.

How to keep ahead

As we have already seen, knowing your customers and helping them to define their needs is one of the main ingredients that will achieve success in keeping at least one step ahead of their information demands. This is especially important when creating an electronic information service, since the ready availability of e-services may mean that your users keep their requirements to themselves under the impression that they can get everything from the web or from desktop information services.

One of the other main ingredients for success is knowing what your customers are planning – how they are going to offer their products and services in future. These may have such an impact on the services that you are currently offering that your own customers may decide to take up the competitors' service.

For example, if you are offering services to a specific group of users such as a research group and you wish to offer e-journals instead of paper-based services, you may find that the e-journal subscription agents decide to contact the research group directly. There is no real reason, if they receive a sufficiently cost-effective offer, why the research group should not take this offer up. They may feel that they would be in control of their own budget and of their choice of journals without having to deal with a 'third party' – your information service. Later in the chapter we shall look at how to deal with this situation.

Your networks

Your professional and personal networks will help you to make your offer of services the most useful and relevant to your users, and ensure that you remain as their first choice for information services.

What are your competitors offering in the way of services?

One way to find out is to ask them! After all, information professionals are a very gregarious bunch, and they will talk informally to others off the record. While you know that they would not divulge confidential information (and surely you would not ask them!) they will often share general information, and perhaps boast a little. You can often identify opportunities to adopt useful services in a way that helps your service without actually stealing anything.

What are competitors planning?

The considerations are similar to those above. However here it would be bad practice to rush to put other people's ideas into practice earlier than they manage to do so!

What is happening in other information centres?

Here the entire world is at your disposal. For your own country, you can no doubt draw upon the professional associations and the whole range of journals that provide news for the sector. While a number of these will carry what are obviously news releases from software and library automation companies, you can see what services have been developed, and you may gain advantage from being an early adopter. For other countries, make sure that you read the various mailing lists (some of these are suggested in the appendices to this book) and look out for anything interesting. Even if the vendor does not operate in your country, you may be able to find the service from another provider, or if the possibility is tempting enough, the vendor may even look for a local agent.

What are e-information services in other sectors offering?

Don't confine your researches to your own sector alone. There may be some ideas in other areas of information work that you can adapt for your own information centre. In some sectors there is considerable investment and new services are often created. That is especially true in the present climate of mergers and rebranding, so – while not everyone is happy about some of the changes – there may be new offers that might be more appropriate to your own areas of work, and to what your customers are doing.

Many organizations have a range of information needs that are not always directly connected to their core business, and providing information services to people with less common requirements is often disproportionately expensive. So it may be that you can afford to buy into a new service from a supplier who has repackaged that information either by adding information that you do require, or by coming up with a new price package that suits you better.

People

People related to your service can be classified in a number of ways. In one way of looking at it, you will have users who are frequent, irregular, or non-users, or those who are information literate or those who need training. You will number suppliers among your contacts, and some of them may be internal suppliers, for example if they contribute to a database. You need to come up with a strategy to keep in touch with all of these.

Are their information needs changing? Do they have plans for different types of work where new services may be important? What are their future plans and how does your service need to adapt to meet their needs?

During your education, training and your various jobs you will have come into contact with a wide range of people from different disciplines and walks of life. Many of them will keep in touch even though they are now working in other countries or organizations. They form an invisible network, an invisible college, who can give you advice or tell you about the latest developments where they are. Many people now have some kind of take on information services, as a user if not as a provider, and their ideas can often help you. Anyway, many of them will be only too pleased to hear from you!

Mentors and gurus

Mentoring can be a formal or informal arrangement that can be of benefit to information specialists. Among the benefits is the possibility to sound out new ideas and thoughts, and expand on them before using them in one's own organization.

In our professional careers we have both had welcome opportunities to present ideas to people at senior levels in the profession and in the organization. They have been able to help to develop plans, and assure us that an idea is workable. However the more senior the position that you reach, the less likely you are to be able to discuss ideas about information services with your peers within the organization. In many cases other senior people have little idea or interest about these areas of work.

There are two points that emerge. One is that you may need to re-develop the relationships that you have with others who now hold senior positions in other organizations as they will better understand the issues that now concern you. In the context of developing e-services, for example, they are very likely to be dealing with issues around electronic service delivery, and the huge cultural changes that this requires in many organizations. The other point is that you may need to identify new mentors who can help with your current concerns. While you will almost certainly want to keep in touch with those who have helped you through the earlier stages of your career, you may well find that, with the best will in the world, they no longer have the understanding that you require of the new issues that you face.

What is the understanding of senior people of the problems that you need to tackle? Can a different network, probably with nothing to do with information management, help you better? (This is possibly the equivalent of 'Should I get out more?' but taking a broad view of the available networks may well suggest that you could profitably meet that old friend who talked of another group where the members had similar backgrounds to your own senior managers. What could these people offer you once they know of your professional interest in electronic services?)

Management

So, we have noted that for a strategic approach to electronic information services in an organization, you will need to manage an approach to the most senior levels. You are likely to need to show them what is possible in order to get their involvement and support for the information service on the financial and communications fronts. Especially for electronic services, the financial aspects are likely to be more difficult than the public relations angles. The business case for electronic services is not obvious, and you will need to produce a convincing argument in favour.

Regular meetings are likely to be a valuable tool which can help to place plans of work for new services into a business context, and equally ensure that plans for the organization take account of the information services' ability to provide appropriate services. All too often parts of an organization are the target of direct sales pitches that end up on the desks of senior management as firm proposals for new business activity involving the unnecessary duplication of electronic information services. Why take out new subscriptions to electronic services when those used by the information service have spare capacity at no additional cost? Why use untrained people to search when there is a professional service that can keep down the costs to the organization as a whole and perhaps broker the take-up of unused time on a subscription service in order to manage costs overall?

Technical

Does your information service manage your organization's computer services department? If not, you will need to ensure that the technical team understand the information services' technical requirements.

We have heard of organizations where the technical services never fully understood what the information team needed – despite, in one example we found, taking people to the USA to show them exactly what was needed, how it had been implemented and the steps that had been taken to set up the necessary network. This took place, of course, in the early days of technological developments for information services. A memorable phrase used by one of the technical people was, 'Yes, it is all technically possible, but we can't do it'. Of course life has become much easier with more reliable software and more robust networks.

An excellent way to achieve good working relations is to use a service level agreement (SLA) as the basis of meetings with the computer services manager and staff. The formal agenda should include work fulfilled in the time between meetings, and performance against the requirements of the SLA. The SLA should be drawn up in conjunction with the computer services department, ensuring a good understanding of responsibilities.

Why an SLA is important

With an SLA, it is essential that all levels of staff are involved in the compilation of the agreement. This is because everyone's personal performance, their understanding of the levels of services to be achieved and the timescales within which these levels of services are to be given are all contained in the agreement. Job descriptions and the required levels of performance will be derived from the SLA through the business-planning process. The job appraisal exercise a year later is not the time to discover that there are problems. So, you need to be aware of the full implications of an SLA at whatever level you are working.

It is often the person working at the enquiry desk, in the interlibrary loans section or the search service section, or in the ordering section who has the most detailed knowledge of the systems that will have to meet any agreements. For instance it is no good agreeing to demands from the technical services department to take down the computer system at a certain time of the day when you and your staff know that this is the peak time for providing services for the users.

Features of an SLA

Service level agreements were first widely used to manage relations with corporate computing sections and have a number of features that reflect their origins. They are often a feature of quality management systems where their precision aids the process of definition of products and services. They clarify the relationship between the supplier and the customer by setting out expectations and responsibilities, and the commitment of both parties to the agreement. Setting out the customer's responsibilities in the contract as well as the supplier's should avoid any arguments that can arise unnecessarily, for example where the customer has more details about a requested document than they actually reveal. Most information workers will have experienced the situation where a customer asks vaguely for some reference only to find that they have all the details in front of them but omitted to tell the information section! The implied suggestion is that it is up to the supplier to find the item required with no further clues. And the SLA is a planning tool for the supplier, by allowing prediction of troughs and peaks of activity.

The SLA is prescriptive, but it should say what is to be done rather than how. To describe and define the required result is useful; to say how things are to be done is unnecessarily restrictive. The supplier should be free to achieve the required result in the best way possible without having to adapt that solution to some local routine that would better be changed to some more efficient way of working.

If a standard service is provided then the agreement need only refer to the standard terms and then list the variations, exceptions or enhancements. This can be particularly useful in the case of electronic services, since many of them are described in standard brochures. The combination of these service descriptions with statements of technical requirements and any variations or exceptions that have been agreed may be all that is needed.

We believe that having an SLA will help everyone involved. The SLA will help people understand issues such as what services are needed, the deadlines to be met, and the necessary steps that should be undertaken when services such as computer services fail. An SLA provides the opportunity to revise the agreements as developments take place, for example when new services become available that are of interest to users of the LIS. The second edition of our book *The complete guide to preparing and implementing service level agreements* (Pantry and Griffiths, 2001) shows in detail how to set up such agreements and equally importantly how to keep the SLA revised.

Winning others across

Because so many people will be involved in creating an e-information service, you will need to win others across at all stages of the creation and maintenance of the service. Get the approval of the organization's senior management to the strategic concept before going out to talk to a range of people in the organization.

Among those you need to contact are:

- The information services staff who will be helping you to implement the service – what are their concerns about electronic services and their role in providing them?
- The other service providers in the organization – what impact do your plans have on them (for example by undercutting an existing service, or by placing additional load on networks)?
- Service providers outside the organization, such as journal suppliers who may need to support the licensing of electronic data, or negotiate new terms – if you do not win these suppliers across, you may find yourself looking at a delay while you re-tender contracts through the European Official Journal.
- Various user groups – your customers may well have an opinion on the services you want to introduce. You may even have to balance the requirements of several groups, e.g. in an academic situation, students and the lecturing staff, or in a business environment the business managers and researchers.

You should also open discussions with known non-users, particularly those in senior positions. Your proposed e-services may well be of benefit to them in alerting users of the service to the organization. You could well attract them with a modern way of delivering information to their workstations. But it is probably easier to start with a clean sheet in creating an e-information service than to move a more traditional information service concept into a fully blown e-information service. Otherwise you may be drawn into arguments about services that have been lost or scaled down.

Whichever is your starting point you will need to have discussions, and both formal and informal meetings, to take people along so that they feel that they have ownership in the creation of the new service. Ask for the opinions of all levels of staff at the outset, so that you do not ignore the needs of managers or of frontline workers, or base your proposals on second-hand accounts of their requirements.

Electronic services seem to raise the emotional stakes when introduced to a workplace. There is suspicion that the services are an excuse to change the nature of people's jobs or even to do away with them, and there is nothing worse than the 'Chinese Whispers' type of rumour where staff do not know what is happening generally or more specifically to them and their jobs.

Staff often have ideas about service management or can describe good practice that they have seen elsewhere, implementation of which would allow them to expand their roles and careers. They will buy in more readily if they have a feeling of involvement in the decisions. Explaining the strategy to people as early as possible will provide the opportunity to delegate parts of the work. Small groups of staff with particular knowledge or interest will be able to develop in particular subject fields or deal with particular suppliers. They will know how to bring in new ideas; and by ensuring that there is a forum where staff can exchange news with other members of the other working groups, you can ensure that everyone keeps in touch with this work.

Using other techniques such as matrix management may help to ensure good working relations and communications. Matrix management cuts across traditional departmental boundaries, thus creating a matrix, and is particularly useful for implementing special projects. Although senior managers may need to arbitrate from time to time, these new ways of working should help to bring out best practice in developing electronic services, and ensure that everyone's knowledge and experience is brought into play.

A final word on the staff front – do ensure that staff representatives are kept fully informed. It's important that they feel comfortable with the proposals, and that you know they understand the potential opportunities as well as dealing with any fears they may have about future job security or changes.

Customers

The customers themselves are perhaps the most difficult groups when it comes to winning their confidence. Many people do not like change, are suspicious of computerized services which do away with the 'comfort blanket' of paper-based services. Again if converting from a traditional service it will necessary to explain at the outset:

- what is planned
- how the changes will be managed
- how the changes will affect customers
- what, if any, training will be needed and
- for whom training will be provided, and how long it will take.

No doubt, if the costs are allocated to their department they will insist on details of any increases. You will need to have your arguments ready to answer questions and deal with any possible dissent. You will be able to describe your customers' current information needs and to demonstrate the cost benefits of moving to an e-information services. Bringing your customers into your confidence at an early stage will strengthen their commitment to you. It should ensure that they refer to you when suppliers and other information services approach them directly and offer services. You could also point out that your understanding of electronic services will probably save them money. Not only will you know how to provide the services within any package at the best value prices by selecting them from the best value source, but you will be able to ensure that the competitor has not cut prices by leaving out any essential but expensive elements!

Keep in touch with your users' current and future needs. They will be increasingly dependent on good-quality information in the future, and will probably be overwhelmed by the sheer volume if they go looking for it themselves on the world wide web.

Suppliers

Your suppliers are another key ally in developing an e-information service that keeps you one step ahead. By maintaining good relations and contacts with them, you will ensure that you are able to get best value in information provision for your users, and be certain that you will remain your users' first port of call when they need improved services. Agents and suppliers are generally willing to help: they know that it will be easier for them to pick up and maintain business if they support your role as the primary broker for information in your organization. Dealing with multiple contact points, not knowing who has authority to order and who will pay, is not the way your average supplier will want to deal with your organization. Your side of the bargain is to make sure that the supplier is not put into a difficult position, so you may need to put your foot down with information cowboys in your business!

Suppliers on the web

In recent years the internet has provided an increasingly important platform for the development of electronic information services. Suppliers and publishers routinely put information on to the internet as a viable means of document supply.

Web-based delivery allows suppliers to offer an enhanced range of services rather than simply providing administrative support such as announcement of publication dates and delays. Full and updated databases are available such as SilverPlatter's Electronic Reference Library (ERL), containing over 300 sources, and Dialog @SiteServer in a range of scientific and technical fields.

Electronic journals

The last five years have seen a huge growth in the range and number of electronic journals available for use by information services and other subscribers. We have seen the growth of integrated services such as SwetsNavigator, and portals like Emerald Library, delivering a wide range of journals and allowing users to navigate to and download articles in formats such as Portable Document Format (.pdf). The agent or publisher thus takes care of much of the day-to-day administration, including handling of permissions and access control.

Services such as this can lead end-users to behave like children let loose in a sweetshop. The sheer quantity of information available can lead them to gorge on uncontrolled amounts of articles and other electronic resources. Information professionals can apply their skills to this mass of information and analyse new materials in order to highlight the most relevant items, which they can suggest to users. The information service thus remains in control of the process, and is ready for any follow-up demands (for example, for copies of articles referred to in the electronic documents). Contents listings can be scrutinized in a similar way, perhaps ensuring that copies of articles in themed issues can quickly be sourced, or that articles by key authors in particular subject fields are added to reference bibliographies. Depending on licensing agreements, copies of key items can be downloaded and added to shared folders.

Using integrated services to head off customer requests

You can make use of vendors' integrated services to head off anticipated user requests. The information centre's life will be easier if you are able to handle the volume of demand for particular items or journals, and e-journals can provide the means to do so. This case study shows how.

Case study

A medium-sized library circulates journals but some key titles can take up to two years since they go to a long list and tend to contain a number of important articles. Many users low down the circulation never see the journal at all, or if it reaches them too many articles are out of date. Nobody knows who has got a particular issue when it is needed in a hurry. The information centre finds itself sending off for British Library Document Supply Centre article copies, or buying extra copies of important journal issues. The solution arrived at in this case might involve keeping the journals in the library, then circulating contents lists containing hyperlinks to an online full-text service. This could show

> reduced costs overall, and ensure that important journals remain available in the information centre. (Since your licence probably demands that you subscribe to the paper version to get electronic access, why not put the paper copies somewhere they can be useful? An unexpected bonus could be greater use of the information centre.)

The administration facilities provided by e-journal suppliers can also help to inform customers without the need for your staff to spend time on dealing with routine enquiries such as the expected arrival date of the next issue of a journal. Suppliers will typically issue bulletins of such information that can be published on an intranet, while some library management systems will allow users to view check-in screens for predicted dates. Other information relating to licensing or costs can also be included on your intranet.

Dealing with particular types of users in organizations

In this and other of our publications we have discussed the different needs of the various user groups in your organization. Our view is that meeting these requirements can be as much an issue of management or of communications as of having particular library and information professional skills.

Senior managers may be intrigued by the opportunities you are developing using e-services, but be ignorant of some of the constraints that you face. Why can't these electronic journals be rolled out to the whole organization, regardless of licences? Why can't the subscription to paper be cancelled now you have all this information? Why does the information centre need so much space in this case?

Information Technology managers may be concerned by the level of demand being placed on their networks, and insist that your services are slowing down access to computing facilities generally, or the performance of the intranet.

Research areas may demand that their most heavily used journals are placed on the network even where costs, licences or technical compatibility may be issues. And so on.

None of these is a show-stopping problem. But they are examples of problems that can be anticipated, like others that will spring to mind in the context of your own organization. You can be ready with financial information such as the details of the increased costs that would be incurred by purchasing further simultaneous user licences. You can obtain some reliable predictions of the additional network load imposed by a particular supplier's service from that supplier. You can discover from agents what technical standards need to be met in order to run a particular product or – for example – to be able to read a particular journal on a Mac rather than a PC.

The same skills and contacts that you use to keep ahead of the customer when dealing with new information services can be used here. The same communications skills that you use when issuing information about the library to users can help you to reinforce the message that your service is on top of all these questions, and thinks ahead.

Summary

In order to manage demand within available resources you need to anticipate customer needs. By offering information and services based on the use of electronic delivery that will meet these requirements, you can gain in several ways:

- Customer requirements are met rapidly by services already tuned to their needs.
- Demand on the information centre is managed within resources: in particular, time pressures are reduced by improved availability of the most requested information.
- Costs can be managed more readily.
- The profile of the information centre as a source of timely, relevant information and its reputation for being in touch with developments in information supply are both enhanced.

To achieve this you will need to involve a range of players, including those we have considered here.

In conclusion

To help you think of ways to change attitudes and perceptions we leave the last words to R. David Lankes, one of the editors of the book *Digital reference service in the new millennium: planning, management and evaluation*, who says:

> I invite you into the revolution. I invite you to be a reference revolutionary. Stop looking at a library as a collection of objects and start seeing it as a house of contexts. Stop looking at librarians as information custodians, and demand they be guides. I invite you to invent the future!

GLOSSARY OF SAMPLE ELECTRONIC SERVICES

We said in the foreword to this book that it is not intended for the people who are currently working on electronic library projects and services, but intended as an introduction to the issues for those information professionals working in smaller communities and organizations who are interested in expanding the range of services available to their customers.

But it needs more than a totally theoretical approach – you need to see some examples at work. Fortunately, a number of electronic library services are available more or less freely on the world wide web, allowing you to see some of the functionality. These sites also often explain the content of the particular service, and set out the eligibility of various types of LIS to join the group. You may find that your community or organization qualifies to take part in these groups, giving you a considerable step forward in building your e-service. Even if it does not, you may get some useful ideas about content, navigation and presentation from looking at these cases.

This selection does not imply any commentary, good or bad, about these projects – simply, these appear to be among the most interesting examples of electronic library and information services at present that can be easily located and seen on the world wide web.

New projects are constantly developing. Apart from the professional press, we suggest that you regularly visit a digital library project portal such as LIBWEB at Berkeley University in order to track projects of interest (**http://sunsite.berkeley.edu/Libweb/**).

Athens

www.athens.ac.uk
www.athens.nhs.uk

Athens is a UK service that provides the higher and further education sector with an access management system for electronic materials. It also provides this service for the NHS through a second version available over the NHSNet and Government Secure Intranet. The technology that manages access for these two groups of users is also available as a commercial product allowing single sign-in access for whatever range of services the organization has arranged access.

Terms of eligibility for access to the National Electronic Library for Health (NeLH) and other elements of the NHS service are to be found at **www.athens.nhs.uk/info/nelheligibility.html**

Incidentally, Athens displays the good practice we mentioned in Chapter 2, since it clearly displays the warning that there is an 'at risk' period for two hours a week while back-ups and maintenance are carried out.

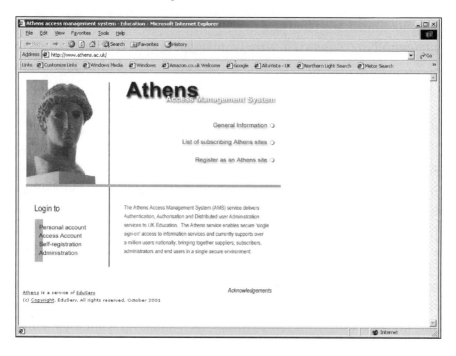

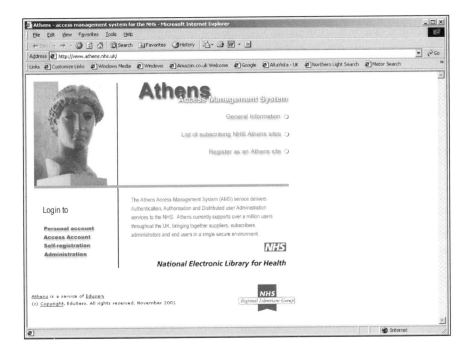

DNER – Distributed National Electronic Resource

www.jisc.ac.uk/dner/

DNER, the Distributed National Electronic Resource, is 'a managed environment for accessing quality assured information resources on the Internet which are available from many sources. These resources include scholarly journals, monographs, textbooks, abstracts, manuscripts, maps, music scores, still images, geospatial images and other kinds of vector and numeric data, as well as moving picture and sound collections.' It consists of a network, content, system management and support, and the interfaces that present the content to the user.

DNER includes a large number of projects – over 50, listed at **www.jisc. ac.uk/dner/development/projects/projects_alphabetical.html** – and a large collection of resources listed at **www.jisc.ac.uk/dner/ collections/licensing.html**

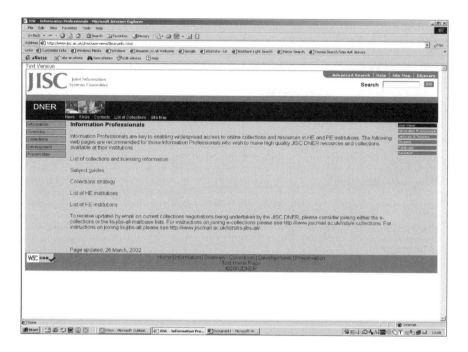

HERON – Higher Education Resources On-Demand

www.heron.ac.uk

HERON describes itself as 'a national service to the UK Higher Education community for copyright clearance, digitisation and delivery of book extracts and journal articles.'

It is developing a bank of digitized materials that are ready for use, subject to copyright clearance. It aims to provide a one-stop shop for copyright clearance and digitization, enabling universities and colleges to provide access to key learning materials for all their students, wherever they are based. HERON is trying to balance the interests of the rights holders with those of the higher education community from which it has grown up, and is aiming to obtain benefits for both groups.

NESLI – National Electronic Site Licensing Initiative

www.nesli.ac.uk

NESLI, the National Electronic Site Licensing Initiative, is a programme, now extended into 2002, to deliver a national electronic journal service to the UK higher education and research community. A consortium consisting of the University of Manchester and Swets Blackwell is taking action to reduce the various barriers (financial, legal and technical) that make take-up of e-services more difficult in the UK higher education sector.

New Library: the People's Network

The report *New Library: the People's Network* was launched in 1997. The eventual outcome was the People's Network – see page 145.

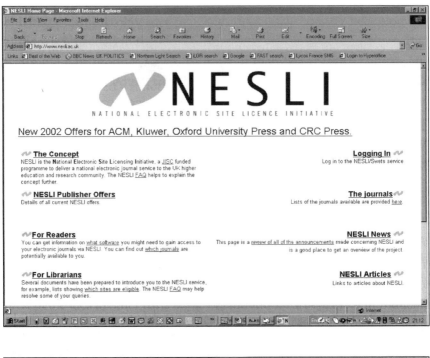

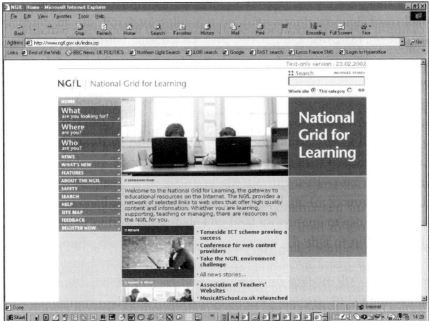

NGfL – the National Grid for Learning

www.ngfl.gov.uk

The National Grid for Learning (NGfL) is the UK Government gateway to educational resources on the internet. It provides a network of selected links to websites that offer high quality content and information.

NeLH – the National Electronic Library for Health

www.nelh.nhs.uk

The ambitious target of the NeLH is to provide a digital library resource for NHS staff, patients and the public. The current set of resources is aimed primarily at staff and researchers, and includes a number of services (such as the Cochrane Library) which are restricted to such groups. However a considerable amount of information is available, and as is clear from the portal style front page, which is considerably fuller with links than

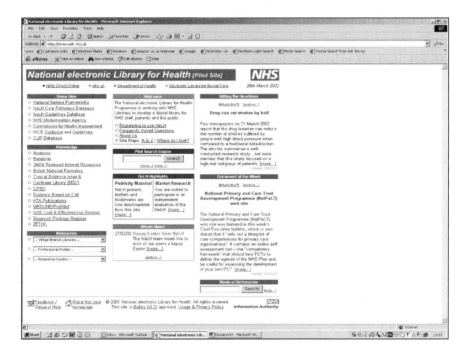

many of our other case studies here, NeLH already provides access to a wide range of resources where patients and the public can browse for medical information. Site navigation gives access to areas such as Knowledge and Know-How, and there are links to other related resources (such as Cochrane, or the Department of Health).

NOF – The New Opportunities Fund

The work of the UK lottery funds distribution agency includes a digitization programme – NOF Digitize **www.nof.org.uk/tempdigit/index.htm**

NOF-Digitize projects are designed to support life-long learning under one of three broad themes; cultural enrichment, citizenship, and re-skilling. A range of materials including text, drawings, photos, maps, film and sound recordings will be converted into electronic formats and enhanced by additional material providing interpretation. Part of the programme is concerned with adopting common standards that will ensure long-term

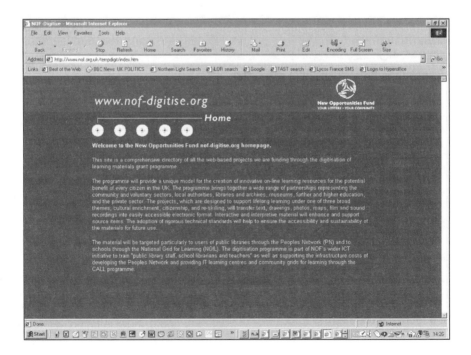

access to the materials. Users in public libraries will have access to the material through the People's Network, while the National Grid for Learning (NGfL) will provide access for users in schools. NOF has a remit to train public library staff, school librarians and teachers in the use of information and communications technology (ICT), and it meets the infrastructure costs of the People's Network as well as providing IT learning centres.

PANDORA – Preserving and Accessing Networked Documentary Resources of Australia

http://pandora.nla.gov.au/index.html

This project is developing policy, guidelines and procedures for the preservation and provision of access to Australian online digital publications. We used the test (proof-of-concept) archive to examine some of the Australian materials quoted in this book. The project has been established to test business principles and technical capability: more than 700 Australian

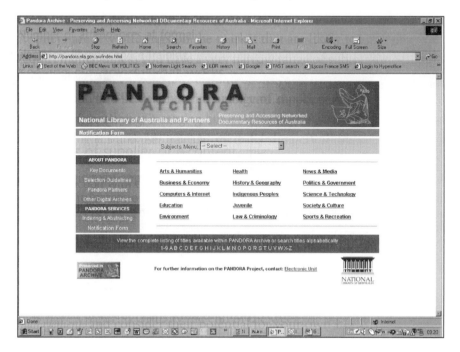

serial and conference titles are available over the world wide web through the catalogue of the National Library of Australia. PANDORA has been offered as a national model and some state libraries are likely to adopt it as a standard for their local digital collections.

PELICAN

www.lboro.ac.uk/departments/dils/disresearch/pelican/indexpage.html

The PELICAN project is intended to develop an understanding of charging mechanisms for distributing commercially published electronic texts to students. It aims to provide a pricing model that can meet the requirements of the various stakeholders in the higher and further education sectors and can clear the way for distributing digitized literature in the academic field.

People's Network

www.peoplesnetwork.gov.uk

The report 'New Library: the People's Network' was launched in 1997. The eventual outcome was the People's Network, which is a project to connect all public libraries to the internet, as part of the Government's commitment to give everyone in the UK the opportunity to get online. Lottery-funded by the New Opportunities Fund and managed by Resource, more than 4000 library centres will be up and running by the end of 2002.

(Library and Information Commission. New Library: the People's Network, London, Library and Information Commission, 1997. Electronic version available free of charge at **www.ukoln.ac.uk/services/lic/newlibrary/contents.html**)

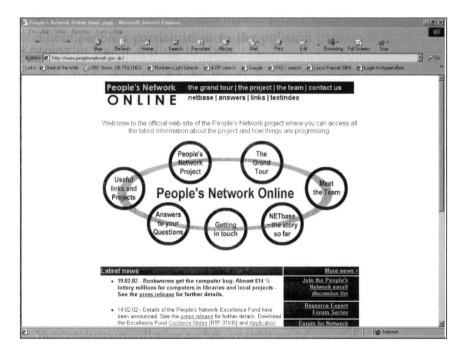

Appendix

REFERENCES AND FURTHER READING

We have listed the references to text quoted in the various chapters and also added other references for those with further curiosity!

Chapter 1   Introducing the concept of the e-information service

Boddy, D., Boonstra, A. and Kennedy, G. (2001) *Managing information systems: an organisational perspective,* Financial Times Prentice Hall (a Pearson Education company), ISBN 0273655957.

Brophy, P. et al. (eds) (2000) *Libraries without walls 4: the delivery of library services to distant users. Proceedings of an international conference organized by CERLIM, 10–14 September 2001,* Facet Publishing, ISBN 185604436X.

Central Computer and Telecommunications Agency (1990) *Managing information as a resource,* HMSO, ISBN 011330529X.

Central Computer and Telecommunications Agency (1993) *Managing supplier relationships: IT Infrastructure Library (ITIL),* HMSO, ISBN 0113305621.

Central Computer and Telecommunications Agency (1994) *Managing contracts for IS/IT services the role of the intelligent customer,* HMSO, ISBN 0113306601.

Central Computer and Telecommunications Agency (1995) *An introduction to managing project risk: management of risk library,* HMSO, ISBN 0113306717.

Central Computer and Telecommunications Agency (1996) *Managing risk to the IS strategy: management of risk library,* HMSO, ISBN 0113306806.

Central Computer and Telecommunications Agency (2000) *SSADM foundation: business systems development with SSADM,* The Stationery Office, ISBN 0113308701.

Covello, J. and Hazelgren, B. J. (1998) *Your first business plan: a simple question and answer format design to help you write your own plan*, 3rd edn, Sourcebooks Trade, ISBN 1570712190.

Covey, S. R. (1999) *The seven habits of highly successful people: restoring the character ethic,* Simon and Schuster, ISBN 0671708635.

The electronic resources acquired by libraries and information centres include: computer software; databases; news feeds; daily financial information sources: see **www.arl.org/scomm/licensing/licbooklet.html**

Gates, K. (2001) Librarians are finding endless opportunities, *Managing Information,* **8** (2), (March), 58.

Goulding, A. et al. (c.2000) *Likely to succeed: attitudes and aptitudes for an effective information profession in the 21st century*, Library and Information Commission research report 8, available at **www.lic.gov.uk/publications/researchreports/index.html/rr8**

Griffiths, P. (2000) The career development of a web officer. In *Managing the virtual branch: public library web managers workshop*, UKOLN, October, available at **www.ukoln.ac.uk/public/events/managing/griffiths/ ukoln%20notes/sld003.htm**

Handy, C. (1989) *The age of unreason*, Business Books Ltd (Century Hutchinson), ISBN 0091740886.

LaGuardia, C. (1998) *Recreating the academic library: breaking virtual ground*, Neal-Schuman Publishers, Inc., ISBN 1555702937.

LaGuardia, C. and Mitchell, B. A. (1998) *Finding common grounds: creating the library of the future without diminishing the library of the past,* Neal-Schuman Publishers, Inc., ISBN 1555702902.

LaGuardia, C. and Vasi, J. (2000) *Designing, building, and teaching in the electronic library classroom*, Neal-Schuman Publishers, Inc., ISBN 1555703801.

Lankes, R. D., Collins, J. W. and Kasowitz, A. S. (eds) (2000) *Digital reference service in the new millennium: planning, management and evaluation*, The New Library Series Number 6, Neal-Schuman Publishers, Inc., ISBN 1555703844.

The book is an easy and exciting read, and contains a useful list of bibliographic references and websites to resources on the topic of digital reference in a variety of contexts. This resource list will be updated regularly online at

www.vrd.org/pubinfo/proceedings99_bib.shtml

Moholt, P. (1985) On converging paths: the computing center and the library, *Journal of Academic Librarianship*, **11** (5), 284–8.

Muirfield, G. (ed.) (1997) *Planning and implementing successful system migrations*, Library Association Publishing, ISBN 1856042189.

Pantry, S. and Griffiths, P. (1998) *Becoming a successful intrapreneur: a practical guide to creating an innovative information service*, Library Association Publishing, ISBN 1856042928.

Pantry, S. and Griffiths, P. (2002) The internal information audit: conducting the audit and implementing the results, *Business Information Review*, **11** (1), in press.

Sayers, R. C. (1999) Some thoughts on strategies for the integration of Reference and Computing/IT service points. In *The virtual reference desk*, CRIG (Caval Reference Interest Group) Forum, July, available at

www.caval.edu.au/parties_and_research/Sayers.html

Shapiro, B. J. and Long, K. B. (1994) Just say yes: re-engineering library user services for the 21st century, *Journal of Academic Librarianship*, **20** (5/6), 285–90.

Taylor, J. (2001) *How to manage information technology projects: a systems approach to managing IT software, hardware, and integration tasks*, McGraw-Hill Publishing Company, ISBN 0814405878.

Tuominen, K. (2000) *Monologue or dialogue in the web environment – the role of networked library and information services in the future: 66th IFLA Council and General Conference, Jerusalem, 13–18 August 2000,* available at

www.ifla.org/IV/ifla66/papers/004-131e.htm

Vickery, J. (2000) *Reorganisation in the British Library to acquire electronic resources: 66th IFLA Council and General Conference, Jerusalem, 13–18 August 2000*, available at
www.ifla.org/IV/ifla66/papers/116-180e.htm

Chapter 2 What kind of an e-information service do you want to provide?

Allen, B. (n.d.) *InfoMapper instructor's guide,* for use with InfoMapper software (but sold separately), Information Management Press, Inc., P.O. Box 19166, Washington, D.C. 20036, USA, ISBN 0960640835.

Basch, R. (1995) *Electronic information delivery – ensuring quality and value*, Gower, ISBN 0566075679.

Batt, C. (1998) *Information technology in public libraries*, Library Association Publishing, ISBN 1856042537.

Bird, J. (1997) *The Reuters guide to good information strategy*, Reuters, ISBN 1901249050.

Burk, C. F. Jr and Horton, F. W. Jr (1991) *InfoMap: the complete guide to discovering corporate information resources*, Prentice-Hall. Now available from Information Management Press, Inc., P.O. Box 19166, Washington, D.C. 20036, USA, ISBN 013464476.

Central Computer and Telecommunications Agency (1990) *Managing information as a resource*, CCTA, HMSO, ISBN 011330529X.
A practical guide showing policy guidelines and how to conduct an information audit. Though oriented to government departments, this slim book is a handy guide. Available from the bookshop at The Stationery Office.

Deegan, M. and Tanner, S. (2001) *Digital futures: strategies for the information age*, Library Association Publishing, ISBN 1856044111.

Gorman, G. E. (2001) *Information services in an electronic environment*, Library Association Publishing, ISBN 1856044033.

Hardy, R. and Oppenheim, C. (2002) Pricing digital progress, *Library Association Record*, **104** (2), (February), 100–1

Henczel, S. (2001) *The information audit: a practical guide*, Information Management Series, K. G. Saur, ISBN 35982436777.

Hildebrand, C. (1995) Information mapping: guiding principles, *CIO: the Magazine for Information Executives*, **8** (18), (July), 60–4.

Higher Education Resources On-Demand, available at
www.heron.ac.uk

Horton, F. W. Jr (1988–9) Mapping Corporate Information Resources, three-part series of articles in the *International Journal of Information Management*, **8** (1988), 249–54; **9** (1989), 19–24; **9** (1989), 91–5.

Horton, F. W. Jr (1991) Infomapping, *The Electronic Library*, **9** (1), (February), 17–19.

Horton, F. W. Jr (n.d.) *The information management workbook: IRM made simple,* 3rd edn, loose-leaf 3-ring binder, Information Management Press, Inc., P.O. Box 19166, Washington, D.C. 20036, USA, ISBN 0960640800.

Hyams, E. (2001) Nursing the evidence: The Royal College of Nursing information strategy, *Library Association Record*, **103** (12), (December), 747–9.

Jantz, Ronald C. (2001) Technological discontinuities in the library: digital projects that illustrate new opportunities for the librarian and the library, *IFLA Journal*, **27** (2), 74–7.

Journal of Knowledge Management, IFS International Ltd, Wolseley Business Park, Kempston, Bedford MK42 7PW, UK.

King, D. W. and Tenopir, C. (2000) *Towards electronic journals* (virtual SLA), Special Libraries Association, available at
www.sla.org/content/Shop/Resources/titlelist/towelecjnl.cfm

Lankes, R. D., Collins, J. W. III and Kasowitz, A. S. (2000) *Digital reference service in the new millennium: planning, management and evaluation*, The New Library Series Number 6, Neal-Schuman Publishers, Inc., ISBN 1555703844.

Lannon, R. (n.d.) *InfoMapper project manager's guide*, for use with InfoMapper software (but sold separately), Information Management Press, Inc., P.O. Box 19166, Washington, D.C. 20036, USA, ISBN 0960640851.

McCracken, C. (2001) Illumination not enumeration: information audits are not a counting exercise but a platform from which to develop a total KM strategy, *Dialog Magazine*, (December), 10–13.

MacLachlan, L. (1996) *Making project management work for you*, Library Association Publishing, ISBN 1856042030.

Ming, D. C. (2000) Access to digital information: some breakthroughs and obstacles, *Journal of Librarianship and Information Science*, **32** (1), 26–32.

Orna, L. (1999) *Practical information policies*, 2nd edn, Gower Press.
This second edition of a book first published in 1990 provides a strategic management perspective on information management and relates it well to knowledge management. A good practical guide with excellent guidance for those developing and implementing information management. This edition has 14 new case studies from the UK, Australia and Singapore.

Owen, T. (2000) *Success at the enquiry desk*, 3rd edn, Library Association Publishing, ISBN 1856044041.

Pan, R. and Higgins, R. (2001) Digitisation projects at Durham University Library – an overview, *Program*, **35** (4), (October), 355–68.

Pantry, S. (ed.) (1999) *Building community networks: strategies and experiences*, Library Association Publishing, ISBN 1856043771.

Pantry, S. and Griffiths, P. (1998) *Becoming a successful intrapreneur: a practical guide to creating an innovative information service*, Library Association Publishing, ISBN 1856042928.

Pantry, S. and Griffiths, P. (2001) *The complete guide to preparing and implementing Service Level Agreements*, 2nd edn, Library Association Publishing, ISBN 1856044106.

Pedley, P. (2002) Resources revealed: tracking down newspapers and journals on the web, *Managing Information*, **9** (1), (January/February), 48–9.
This article suggests a number of websites that can help users to locate the sites of newspapers and journals, or at least the details of who publishes them.

Pinchot, G. (1985) *Intrapreneuring: why you don't have to leave the corporation to become an entrepreneur*, Harper and Row.

Rees-Jones, L. and Kidd, T. (eds) (2000) *The serials management handbook: a practical guide to print and electronic serials management*, Library Association Publishing, ISBN 185604355X.

Reuters Business Information (1996) *Dying for information? An investigation into the effects of information overload in the UK and worldwide*, Reuters Business Information, available at
http://about.reuters.com/rbb/research/dying.htm

Reuters; Ronin Research Services (1997) *Glued to the screen: an investigation into information addiction worldwide*, Reuters, ISBN 0901249068.

Smith, K. (1999) *Delivering reference services to users outside the library*, Paper *presented to: 1999 & Beyond: Partnerships & Paradigms, Sydney, September 1999*, available at
www.csu.edu.au/special/raiss99/papers/ksmith.html

Tanner, S. (2001) Librarians in the digital age – planning digitisation projects, *Program*, **35** (4), (October), 327–37.

TFPL Ltd (1999) *Skills for knowledge management: a briefing paper*, based on research undertaken by TFPL on behalf of The Library and Information Commission, LIC. Executive summary and also full text available at
www.lic.gov/publications/index.html

Marketing

Coote, H. and Batchelor, B. (1998) *How to market your library service effectively*, 2nd edn, Aslib, ISBN 0851423965.

Elliott de Sáez, E. (2002) *Marketing concepts for libraries and information services*, 2nd edn, Library Association Publishing, ISBN 0851574483.

Hamilton, F. (1990) *Infopromotion*, Gower, ISBN 0566055775.

Hart, K. (1998) *Marketing your information services*, Library Association Publishing, ISBN 1856041824.

Leigh, A. and Maynard, M. (1993) *Perfect communications: all you need to get it right first time*, Random House, ISBN 0099410060.

Library Association (1997) *Marketing library and information services: LA training package*, Library Association Publishing, ISBN 185604274X.

Software

InfoMapper software package, IBM-compatible standalone PC version (Release 1.2 Mod. 1). LAN version also available, as well as French, Spanish and German language IBM-compatible PC versions. Information Management Press, Inc., P.O. Box 19166, Washington, D.C. 20036, USA, available from Information Mapping, Inc., 411 Waverley Oaks Road, Waltham MA 02452-8470, USA, Tel: +1 781 906-6400 or (800) INFOMAP (463-6627) – see **www.infomap.com Email: inquiry@infomap.com** (also European and South African associates).

Subscription agents

The major subscription agents usually provide their users with access to bibliographic databases containing details of journals, their ISSNs, frequency, publisher and other details. Check the website of the Association of Subscription Agents for a listing of many subscription agents (**www. subscription-agents.org**), but here are some of the major ones:

Blackwell Publishing Synergy online service
    www.blackwell-synergy.com
Ebsco
    www.ebsco.com
Everetts
    www.everett.co.uk
Otto Harrassowitz
    www.harrassowitz.de
Prenax
    www.prenax.com
Rowecom
    www.rowe.com
SwetsBlackwell
    www.swetsblackwell.com
TDNet
    www.tdnet.com

Chapter 3   Where are the customers?

Akeroyd, J. (2001) The management of change in electronic libraries, *IFLA Journal,* **27** (2), 70–3.

Borgman, C. (1986) Why are online catalogues hard to use?, *Journal of ASIS,* **37** (6), 387–400.

Borgman, C. (1996) Why are online catalogues still hard to use?, *Journal of ASIS,* **47** (7), 493–503, available at
www.sims.berkeley.edu/courses/is202/f01/borgman.pdf

Goodman, D. (2002) A year without print at Princeton, and what we plan next, *Learned Publishing,* **15** (1), (January), 43–50.

Griffiths, J.-M. (1999) Why the web is not a library, *FID review,* **1** (1), 13–20.

Jacquesson, A. (2000) De la difficulté à utiliser les bibliothèques numériques, *Bulletin d'Information [Association des Bibliothécaires Français],* **188**, (3e trimestre), available at
www.abf.asso.fr/publications/bulletin/188/article2.html

Jantz, R. (2001) E-books and new library service models: an analysis of the impact of e-book technology on academic libraries, *Information Technology and Libraries,* **20** (2), 104–112.

Jatkevicius, J. et al. (2000) Free legal resource aggregators on the web, *Econtent,* **23** (5), (October/November), 27–34.

Law, D. (1997) Parlour games: the real nature of the internet, *Serials,* **10** (2), July 1997.

Muet, F. (1999) Services et revues électroniques dans l'enseignement supérieur: synthèse de quelques enquêtes récentes sur les usages, *Bulletin des Bibliothèques de France,* **44** (5), 18–23.

Pinfield, S. (2001) Managing electronic library services; current issues in UK higher education institutions, *Ariadne,* 29, available at
www.ariadne.ac.uk/issue29/pinfield/intro.html

Quigley, B. (2000) Physics databases and the Los Alamos e-Print Archive, *Econtent,* **23** (5), (October/November), 22–6.

Rusbridge, C. (1998) Towards the hybrid library, *D-Lib Magazine,* (July/August), available at

www.d-lib.org/dlib/july98/rusbridge/07rusbridge.html

Rusbridge, C. and Royan, B. (2000) *Towards the hybrid library: developments in UK higher education, 66th IFLA Council and General Conference, Jerusalem, 13–18 August 2000*. available at
www.ifla.org/IV/ifla66/papers/001-142e.htm

Smith, K. (1999) *Delivering reference services to users outside the library. Paper presented to 1999 and beyond: partnerships and paradigms. RAISS Conference, Sydney, 6–8 September 1999*, Reference and Information Services Section, Australian Library and Information Association.

Special Libraries Association. Special Committee on Competencies for Special Librarians (1996) *Competencies for special librarians of the 21st century: full report, submitted to the SLA Board of Directors by Joanne Marshall, Chair; Bill Fisher; Lynda Moulton; and Roberta Piccoli*, SLA, available at
www.sla.org/content/SLA/professional/meaning/competency.cfm

Websites

e-brary
www.ebrary.com
Lucent Technology Foundation
www.lucent.com
Press release about the Partnership in Global Learning, available at
www.lucent.com/press/0300/000309.coa.html
Partnership in Global Learning
http://grove.ufl.edu/~pgl/

Chapter 4   What kind of information do your customers need?

Australian Library and Information Association (1997) *NT libraries serve diverse people in remote locations*, press release, 4 May 1997, for Australian Library Week, ALIA, available at
www.alia.org.au/press.releases/1997.05.04c.html

Brown, D. J. (2001) The impact of disintermediation and the new economy on STM electronic information systems, *Serials,* **14** (1), (March), 47–55.

Chu, H. (2000) Promises and challenges of electronic journals: academic libraries surveyed, *Learned Publishing,* **33** (3), (July), 169–75.

Clegg, B. (2001) *The professional's guide to mining the internet, information gathering and research on the net,* 2nd edn, Kogan Page, ISBN 0749435557.

Deconinck, C. and Gauchet, P. (1998) Gravelines Grand-Fort Philippe (Nord): deux approches différentes de l'exploitation d'intranet, *Bulletin d'Informations, [Association des Bibliothécaires Français],* **184-5** (3e–4e trimestre).

Dorr, J. and Akeroyd, R. (2001) New Mexico tribal libraries, *Computers in Libraries,* **21** (9), (October), 36–42.

A grant from the Bill & Melinda Gates Foundation has funded the Native American Access to Technology Program.

Gordon, A. C., Gordon, M. T. and Moore, E. J. (2001) *Library patrons heavily use public access computers & other library services, and want more: a report to the Bill & Melinda Gates Foundation U.S. Library Program on a survey of library patrons in five states,* Public access to computing project, Evans School of Public Affairs, University of Washington, available at **www.gatesfoundation.org/libraries/uslibraryprogram/evaluation/ patron_501.pdf**

International Standards Organization (1998) ISO 23950: 1998 Information and documentation – Information retrieval

(Z39.50) –– Application service definition and protocol specification, ISO.

King, D. W. and Tenopir, C. (2002) Scholarly journal and digital database pricing: threat or opportunity? In MacKie-Mason, J. and Lougee, W. J. (eds), *Bits and bucks: economics and usage of digital collection,* MIT Press.

Lankes, D. et al. (eds) (2000) *Digital reference service in the new millennium: planning, management and evaluation,* The New Library Series Number 6, Neal-Schuman Publishers, Inc. ISBN 1555703844.

The book is an easy and exciting read, and contains a useful list of bibliographic references and websites to resources on the topic of digital reference in a variety of contexts. This resource list will be updated regularly online at

www.vrd.org/pubinfo/proceedings99_bib.html

Library and Information Commission (1997) *New library: the people's network*, UKOLN for the LIC, available at
www.ukoln.ac.uk/services/lic/newlibrary/

Miller, P. (1999) Z39.50 for all, *Ariadne*, **21** (September), available at
www.ariadne.ac.uk/issue21/23950/

O'Flynn, S. (2001) Giving them what they want, *Information World Review*, (September), 28.

Owen, T. (2000) *Success at the enquiry desk*, 3rd edn, Library Association Publishing, ISBN 1856044041.

Pantry, S. and Griffiths, P. (1998) *Becoming a successful intrapreneur: a practical guide to creating an innovative information service*, Library Association Publishing, ISBN 1856042928.

Pantry, S. and Griffiths, P. (2001) *The complete guide to preparing and implementing Service Level Agreements*, 2nd edn, Library Association Publishing, ISBN 1856044106.

Reuters Business Information (1996) *Dying for information? An investigation into the effects of information overload in the UK and worldwide*, Reuters Business Information, available at
http://about.reuters.com/rbb/research/dying.htm

Reuters; Ronin Research Services (1997) *Glued to the screen: an investigation into information addiction worldwide*, Reuters, ISBN 0901249068.

Tenopir, C. and King, D. W. (2001) Lessons for the future of journals, *Nature*, **413** (6857), (18 October), 672–4.
The message is that science journals provide major benefits and will continue to thrive.

Tenopir, C. et al. (2001) Scientists' use of journals: differences (and similarities) between print and electronic, *National Online 2001: proceedings*, Information Today Inc, 469–82.

Vandevelde, H. (2002) Customer care is on the menu, *Sunday Times*, (10 February), 79.

Chapter 5   Who needs to be involved in your plans?

Inger, S. (2001) The importance of aggregators, *Learned Publishing*, **14** (4), (October), 287–90.

Discussion groups

The Washington Library Research Consortium (WRLC) maintains a list of mainly US discussion lists of interest to the LIS profession:
www.wrlc.org/LiblistsQueries/SDetail.idc?SubID=8
It includes the useful 'Liblicense-l' list:
www.library.yale.edu/~llicense/

In the UK, JISCMail hosts 25 lists of interest in this area, many of them open to all readers, listed at
www.jiscmail.ac.uk/category/P2.html
Of these, LIS-e-journals and LIS-e-books are probably of most interest to readers of this book.

Major francophone resources are listed at
www.francopholistes.com/espaces/metiers/documentalistes.shtml
They include the discussion lists of the main French and Belgian professional bodies (ADBS and ADB-VDB) and two widely used lists biblio-fr (**http://listes.cru.fr/wws/arc/biblio-fr**) and Resonet which publishes a fairly regular e-bulletin (**http://actu.ladoc.net/**).

German resources as well as several English and French language projects are listed at
www.bib-info.de/komm/knt_neu/fundgrub/bib_dig.htm

A list of digital library resources is maintained by *Google* at
http://directory.google.com/Top/Reference/Libraries/Digital/

Chapter 6   Budgeting for your e-information service

Albany University on the Developing National Library Network Statistics & Performance Measures project

www.albany.edu/~imlsstat/

Ball, D. and Pye, J. (1999) Library purchasing consortia in the UK: activity and practice, *Library and Information Briefings*, **88**, 1–15.

Ball, D. and Pye, J. (2000) Library purchasing consortia: the UK periodicals supply market, *Learned Publishing*, **13** (1), (January).

Ball, D. and Wright, S. (2000) Procuring electronic information: new business models, *Library Consortium Management: An International Journal*, **2** (7), 145–58.

Bertot, J. C., McClure, C. R. and Ryan, J. (1999) *Developing national public library statistics: performance measures for the networked environment: analysis of State Library data elements for networked information resources and services*, available at

http://www.albany.edu/~imlsstat/state.analysis.pdf

Bevan, S. (2001) Replacing print with e-journals – can it be done? A case study, *Serials*, **14** (1), (March), 17–24.

Boyle, F. (2001) Veni vidi non vici: e-journals management at the University of Liverpool, *Serials*, **14** (1), (March), 25–32.

Brennan, P., Hersey, K. and Harper, G. (1997) *Licensing electronic resources: strategic and practical considerations for signing electronic information delivery agreements*, US Association Research Libraries, available at

www.arl.org/scomm/licensing/licbooklet.html

Brophy, P. (2001) Electronic library performance indicators: the EQUINOX project, *Serials*, **14** (1), (March), 5–9.

Brophy, P. and Wynne, P. M. (1997) *Management information systems and performance measurement for the electronic library: eLib Supporting Study (MIEL2) MIEL (Management Information in Electronic Libraries) final report*, available at

www.ukoln.ac.uk/dlis/models/studies/mis/mis.rtf

Building relationships with supplies (themed issue), *The TQM Magazine*, **5** (5), (October), 1993.

Byrd, S. et al. (2001) Cost/benefit analysis for digital library projects: the Virginia Historical Inventory Project, *The Bottom Line: Managing Library Finances,* **14** (2), 65–75.

Cornford, J. (2001) A costing model for a hybrid library shell, *Library Management*, **22** (1/2), 37–8.

Duncan, M. (1997) The electronic library at work, *Managing Information*, **4** (5), (June), 31–4.

ESYS Consulting (2001) *Summative evaluation of phase 3 of the e-Lib initiative: final report*, ESYS, Section 5.2, 50.

The EQUINOX project, funded by the Telematics for Libraries programme funded by the European Commission, has developed a set of proposed performance indicators for electronic libraries (**http://equinox.dcu.ie/ reports/pilist.html**).

Falk, H. (1999) Projecting the library onto the web, *Electronic Library*, **17** (6), (December), 395–9.

Fialkoff, F. (2001) Rising costs and netLibrary, *Library Journal*, (15 December). Also available at
www.libraryjournal.com

GALILEO Planet (Winter 2002), 1, available at
www.usg.edu/galileo/planet/planet_winter_draft3_final.pdf

Griffiths, P. (2000) *Managing your internet and intranet services: the information and library professional's guide to strategy*, Library Association Publishing, ISBN 1856043401.

Gyeszly, S. D. (2001) Electronic or paper journals? Budgetary development and user satisfaction questions, *Collection Building*, **20** (1), 5–10.

ICOLC, the International Coalition of Library Consortia (2001) *Guidelines for statistical measures of usage of web-based information resources*, rev. edn, available at
www.library.yale.edu/consortia/2001webstats.htm

Landesman, M. (2001) The cost of reference, *Library Journal*, reference supplement, (15 November). Also available at
www.libraryjournal.com

Law, C. (2000) *PANDORA – towards a national collection of selected Australian online publications. Paper given to IFLA, 66th IFLA Council and general conference, Jerusalem, 13–18 August 2000*, available at
www.ifla.org/IV/ifla66/papers/174-157e.htm

McCracken, C. (2001) Illumination not emuneration: information audits are not a counting exercise but a platform from which to develop a total KM strategy, *Dialog Magazine*, (December), 10–13.

Marunet e-services supply arm
www.maruzen.co.jp/home-eng/marunet.html#3

Pantry, S. and Griffiths P. (1998) *Becoming a successful intrapreneur: a practical guide to creating an innovative information service*, Library Association Publishing, ISBN 1856042928.

Pantry, S. and Griffiths, P. (2001) *The complete guide to preparing and implementing service level agreements,* 2nd edn, Library Association Publishing, ISBN 1856044106.

Pantry, S. and Griffiths, P. (2002) The internal information audit: conducting the audit and implementing the results, *Business Information Review,* **19** (1), (March).

Pascoe, R. and Black, H. M. (2001) Virtual libraries – long overdue: the Digital Agenda Act and Australian libraries, *Australian Library Journal*, **50** (2), available at
www/alia.org.au/alj/50.2/full.txt/virtual.libraries.html

Pinfield, S. (2001) *Beyond e-lib: lessons from Phase 3 of the Electronic Libraries programme*, available at
www.ukoln.ac.uk/services/elib/papers/other/pinfield-elib/ elibreport.pdf

Rusbridge, C. and Royan, B. (2000) *Towards the hybrid library: developments in UK higher education. Paper given at IFLA, 66th IFLA Council and general conference, Jerusalem, 13–18 August 2000*, available at
www.ifla.org/IV/ifla66/papers/001-142e.htm

Sloan, B. (n.d.) *Library consortia documents online*, University of Illinois at Urbana–Champaign, available at
www.lis.uiuc.edu/~b-sloan/consort.htm
The Graduate School of Library and Information Science provides a collection of useful documents for the establishment and management of such groups.

Spiteri, A. (2001) Unpublished presentation on Elsevier services during session 'Les enjeux économiques et culturels de la numérisation', 18th IDT conference, Palais des Congrès, Paris, 29–31, May 2001.

Vickery, J. (2000) *Reorganisation in the British Library to acquire electronic resources. Paper given at IFLA, 66th IFLA Council and general conference, Jerusalem, 13–18 August 2000*, available at
www.ifla.org/IV/ifla66/papers/116-180e.htm

Woodward, H. (2001) *Usage statistics. Presentation to the e-ICOLC conference, Espoo Meripuisto, Finland, November 2001*, available at
www.lib.helsinki.fi/finelib/eicolc/Woodward.ppt

Managing suppliers

Ball, D. and Pye, J. (1999) Library purchasing consortia in the UK: activity and practice, *Library and Information Briefings,* **88**, 1–15.

Building relationships with suppliers (1993) *The TQM Magazine*, (themed issue), **5** (5), (October).

CPI Ltd. (1998) *Changing relationships: new dimensions in library supply: proceedings of a seminar held in December 1998*, CPI Ltd, ISBN 1898869499.

Eden, R. (1998) Bookfund tendering, assessment and evaluation – the librarian's viewpoint, *Taking Stock*, 7–11.

Gambles, B. (2000) Procurement: new skills for best value?, *Library and Information Appointments,* **3** (17), App. (August), 373–4.

Greenhalgh, N. (1993) *Managing supplier relationships*, HMSO.

Hardwood, P. and Prior, A. (1998) The role and service of subscription agents, *Library and Information Briefings*, **81**, 2–12.

Inger, S. (2001) The importance of aggregators, *Learned Publishing,* **14** (4), (October), 287–90.

Lancaster, N. (1998) Bookfund tendering, assessment and evaluation – the supplier's viewpoint, *Taking Stock*, 1–6.

Naylor, C. (2000) When the supplier selects, *Bookseller*, (18 February), 28–9.

Naylor, C. (2000) Liverpool scores with supplier selection, *Bookseller*, (2 June), 28–9.

Pye, J. and Ball, D. (1999) *Library purchasing consortia in the UK: activity benefits and practice*, CPI Ltd.

Sidebottom, D. (1998) Tendering for library services and supplies, *Serials*, **11** (3), (November), 224–5.

Wootton, D. (1999) Managing your service suppliers, *Managing Information*, **6** (4), (May), 41–3.

Managing e-suppliers

Bates, M. E.(1998) How to implement electronic subscriptions: replacing the routing list hassle, *Online,* (May), 80–6.

Lister Cheese, A. (2000) *Electronic information resources from Swets Blackwell. Paper given at e-OSHE World: Seeing the Future Conference, Dublin, Ireland, Friday 23 June 2000*, available at
**www.aposho.org/BBS/KOSHA.pphp3/SwetsBlackwell.ppt?act=
read&preact=down&rowid=7**
e-mail: Alistercheese@uk.swetsblackwell.com

Percy, R. (1997) *Library services managing successful outsourcing in the digital age. Paper given at Digital library technology 97: transforming library services for the digital age – meeting user needs for electronic information delivery, IES Conference, Chatswood, NSW, Australia*, 207–21.

Chapter 7   Keeping in touch with your customers

Deconinck, C. and Gauchet, P. (1998) Gravelines Grand-Fort Philippe (Nord): deux approches différentes de l'exploitation d'intranet, *Bulletin d'Informations, [Association des Bibliothécaires Français]*, **184-5**, (3e–4e trimestre).

International Standards Organization, *ISO 9004:2000 Quality Management for Services: performance improvements* and *ISO 9001:2000 Quality Management Requirements*, ISO.

Leigh, A. and Maynard, M. (1997) *Perfect communications: all you need to get it right first time*, Random House, ISBN 0099410060.

Smith, K. (1999) *Delivering reference services to users outside the library. Paper*

presented to 1999 and Beyond: Partnerships and Paradigms, Sydney, September 1999, available at
www.csu.edu.au/special/raiss99/papers/ksmith.html

Chapter 8   Keeping one step ahead of your competitors

Covey, S. R. (1999) *The seven habits of highly successful people: restoring the character ethic,* 3rd edn, Simon and Shuster, ISBN 0671708635

Lankes, D. et al. (eds) (2000) *Digital reference service in the new millennium: planning, management and evaluation*, The New Library Series Number 6, Neal-Schuman Publishers, Inc., ISBN 1555703844.

The book is an easy and exciting read, and contains a useful list of bibliographic references and websites to resources on the topic of digital reference in a variety of contents. This resource list will be updated regularly online at
www.vrd.org/pubinfo/proceedings99_bib.html

Pantry, S. and Griffiths P. (1998) *Becoming a successful intrapreneur: a practical guide to creating an innovative information service*, Library Association Publishing, ISBN 1856042928.

Pantry, S. and Griffiths, P. (2001) *The complete guide to preparing and implementing service level agreements*, 2nd edn, Library Association Publishing, ISBN 1856044106.

Glossary of sample electronic services

This section includes references that describe the featured projects in more detail, as well as references to other projects of interest.

Bley, R. and McIntyre, R. (1999) NESLI – the National Electronic Site Licence Initiative, *VINE,* **110**, (July), 34–7, available at
www.nesli.ac.uk/vine2.html

Brophy, P. (2001) *The library in the twenty-first century: new services for the information age*, Library Association Publishing, ISBN 1856043754

See in particular Chapter 5, What is a library: digital and hybrid libraries.

Hampson, A. (2001) Practical experiences of digitization in the BUILDER hybrid library project, *Program*, **35** (3), (July), 263–75.

Higher Education Resources On-Demand
www.heron.ac.uk

Law, C. (2000) *PANDORA – towards a national collection of selected Australian online publications. Paper given at 66th IFLA Council and General Conference, Jerusalem, 13–18 August 2000*, available at
www.ifla.org/IV/ifla66/papers/174-157e

Library and Information Commission (1997) *New Library: the People's Network*, Library and Information Commission, available at
www.ukoln.ac.uk/services/lic/newlibrary/contents.html

NHS Information Authority (2000) *National electronic Library for Health*, NHS Information Authority.

NHS Information Authority (2000) *NELH-PC: primary care National electronic Library for Health*, NeLH-PC Project Team, NHS Information Authority.

NOVEL (New York Online Virtual Electronic Library): libraries expanding information access for New Yorkers in the 21st century' (2001) [NOVEL Planning Team], available at
ftp://unix2.nysed.gov/pub/state.lib.pubs/novel/finalpln.pdf

Pinfield, S. and Dempsey, L. (2001) The Distributed National Electronic Resource (DNER) and the hybrid library, *Ariadne*, (January), 26, available at
www.ariadne.ac.uk/issue26/dner/intro.html

Prior, A. (1999) NESLI – progress through collaboration, *Learned Publishing*, **12** (1), (January), available at
www.nesli.ac.uk/alpsp.html

Woodhouse, S. (2001) The People's Network and the learning revolution: building the NOF digitise programme, *Ariadne*, **29**, (October), available at
www.ariadne.ac.uk/issue29/woodhouse/intro.html

INDEX

Building an Electronic Resource Collection: a practical guide

STUART D. LEE

Despite increasing library expenditure on large electronic resources, or datasets, very little help is available to those involved in acquiring them. All information and library professionals involved with collection development are currently confronting the challenge of how to make informed decisions in the face of the bewildering array of electronic resources available.

This practical book addresses this situation by guiding the information professional step-by-step through building and managing an electronic resource collection. It outlines the range of electronic products currently available in abstracting and indexing, bibliographic, and other services – such as OCLC products, Web of Science, e-journals, etc. – and then describes how to effectively select, evaluate and purchase them.

Invaluable insights are given into e-collection planning and budgeting implications, and a system is proposed for coping with this increasingly important area. The case studies and models used are fully international in their application. Issues covered include:

- What is a dataset? Why buy one?
- Formulating an electronic collection development policy
- What is on offer? The electronic resources landscape
- E-journals and e-books
- What should one buy? Assessing and acquiring the dataset
- How does one deliver the dataset? Networking, user interfaces, usage statistics.

This invaluable guide identifies best practice and highlights the pitfalls involved in building an electronic resource collection. It includes a select bibliography of journals and e-mail lists, articles, monographs and reports for further reading. This is an essential book for the professional or student new to e-collection development, as well for the experienced practitioner.

Stuart D. Lee MA PhD is Head of the Learning Technologies Group at Oxford University Computing Services.

2002; 160pp; paperback; 1-85604-422-X; £24.95

E-learning and Teaching in Library and Information Services

BARBARA ALLAN

Online learning is becoming an increasingly important approach to user education, information literacy and ILS staff development. ILS staff are becoming increasingly involved in the business of e-learning and teaching, from designing and developing materials and programmes through to supporting individual and group learning using virtual learning environments.

This book provides an overview and guide to the rapidly developing field of virtual learning environments, and provides much-needed practical guidance to the development, use and delivery of online learning and teaching materials and programmes. It is presented in a readable and visually attractive style, including ready-to-use aids such as checklists, questionnaires, charts and tables. It also includes a wide range of case studies in an ILS context, taken from current practice of the information and library world in the UK and worldwide. Key areas covered include:

- models of online learning and teaching
- the internet and web: using learning resources
- virtual learning environments
- electronic assessment
- basic conferencing skills for tutors
- managing online learning and teaching
- moving from conventional learning and teaching to online.

This book is essential reading for anyone interested in online learning and teaching ideas, particularly library and information staff involved in online learning and training, as well as students on information and library course.

Barbara Allan BSc MA MSc PGCE MCLIP is an independent trainer and author. Her previous experience includes managing academic and workplace libraries.

2002; 224pp; paperback;1-85604-439-4; £34.95

Getting and Staying Noticed on the Web
Your web promotion questions answered

PHIL BRADLEY

Now that so much information is communicated via the internet, it has become essential for any library or information service to promote itself on the web by creating its own website.

This exciting new book tells you everything you could possibly need to know about how to promote your website so that it really gets noticed. Written by the author of the successful The advanced internet searcher's handbook, it will guide you through all the stages needed to plan a successful promotion strategy for your website, from the initial planning and technical challenges involved in setting up the site right through to the important ongoing tasks of maintaining the website and monitoring its success.

This easy-to-read question and answer style handbook explains web promotion specifically as it relates to websites in the library and information world. The author has wide practical experience in this field and knows exactly the right questions that need to be asked. The following key areas are covered:

- first steps
- design issues
- search engines
- images
- up and running
- interactivity
- using mailing lists and newsgroups
- banners
- traditional promotion services
- press releases
- viral marketing
- the competition
- monitoring success
- further resources.

If you are responsible for the delivery and promotion of a successful website – you need this book!

Phil Bradley has a background as an information professional and is currently an independent internet consultant.

2002; 224pp; paperback; 1-85604-455-6; £29.95

Libraries Without Walls 4
The delivery of library services to distant users

PETER BROPHY, SHELAGH FISHER AND ZOË CLARKE, EDITORS FOR CERLIM

Distributed learning is becoming a reality throughout the world, requiring that learning opportunities and materials are delivered to citizens in their locality, at home or at work. The concept of the 'library without walls' is no longer a theoretical perspective but is being implemented across the world in many different ways to meet the needs of many different users. The almost universal adoption of information and communications technologies (ICTs) among libraries, coupled with the use of the world wide web as a delivery vehicle, means that more and more users are accessing services remotely. The implications for this 'disintermediation' of library services are profound.

This edited collection brings together the proceedings of the fourth Libraries Without Walls Conference organized by CERLIM, held in 2001, which addressed the key strategic issues arising from international, regional and cross-sectoral approaches to the provision of library services to distant users. Papers written by leading professionals worldwide are grouped under the following themes:

- libraries and virtual learning environments
- online enquiry services for remote users
- virtual libraries and national initiatives
- user behaviour and user training in the distributed environment
- the public library's role in serving distant users
- content development for the virtual environment
- key technology issues in delivering services to distant users.

These state-of-the-art papers will enable library managers and information professionals in all sectors to keep abreast of the latest developments in this vital area. The book will also assist educational specialists and course developers in increasing their understanding of the role and importance of information in the learning process.

2002; 320pp; cased jacketed; 1-85604-436-X; £39.95